The Literature of Cinema

ADVISORY EDITOR: **MARTIN S. DWORKIN**
INSTITUTE OF PHILOSOPHY AND POLITICS OF EDUCATION
TEACHER'S COLLEGE, COLUMBIA UNIVERSITY

THE LITERATURE OF CINEMA presents a comprehensive selection from the multitude of writings about cinema, rediscovering materials on its origins, history, theoretical principles and techniques, aesthetics, economics, and effects on societies and individuals. Included are works of inherent, lasting merit and others of primarily historical significance. These provide essential resources for serious study and critical enjoyment of the "magic shadows" that became one of the decisive cultural forces of modern times.

How to Appreciate Motion Pictures

Edgar Dale

ARNO PRESS & THE NEW YORK TIMES

New York • 1970

109196

Reprint Edition 1970 by Arno Press Inc.
Library of Congress Catalog Card Number: 70-124027
ISBN 0-405-01645-X
ISBN for complete set: 0-405-01600-X
Manufactured in the United States of America

HOW TO APPRECIATE
MOTION PICTURES

HOW TO APPRECIATE
MOTION PICTURES

A MANUAL OF MOTION–PICTURE CRITICISM
PREPARED FOR HIGH–SCHOOL STUDENTS

BY

EDGAR DALE

RESEARCH ASSOCIATE, BUREAU OF EDUCATIONAL RESEARCH
OHIO STATE UNIVERSITY

NEW YORK

THE MACMILLAN COMPANY

1937

PREFACE

IN the Spring of 1929 the Payne Fund of New York City made available funds for the scientific study of the effect of motion pictures on youth. These studies were made by the Committee on Educational Research of the Payne Fund at the request of the National Committee for the Study of Social Values in Motion Pictures, now the Motion Picture Research Council, 366 Madison Avenue, New York City. It was decided at the same time that a constructive program of teaching youth to develop higher standards of taste in motion pictures was desirable. The writer was given the task of preparing teaching materials for this purpose.

The first task attempted in connection with this project was that of discovering the standards of excellence set up by reviewers of motion pictures. In general, this project proved fruitless, since the motion-picture critics of today, with few exceptions, present little in their reviews other than a statement of the story and the reviewer's personal likes or dislikes in reference to the picture.

Much assistance, however, was secured from the few available books on motion-picture criticism, such as: *The Film Till Now*, by Paul Rotha; *The New Spirit in the Cinema*, by Huntly Carter; *Scenario and Screen*, by Frances Taylor Patterson. Welford Beaton's *Hollywood Spectator* proved an excellent source of information on standards by which to evaluate current motion pictures. Foreign publications such as *Close-Up* and the *Cinema Quarterly* offered fundamental data on film techniques.

The problem of translating technical material, written for adults interested in this field, into reading materials satisfactory for high-school students was a difficult one to solve. The method adopted was that of writing the book, mimeographing it, securing criticisms from the pupils who read it and the teachers who taught the materials, and revising it again. To secure satisfactory results the book was put through three mimeographed editions, an experimental printed edition, and the present commercial edition.

The results of the investigations reported in companion volumes in this series demonstrate conclusively the effect of the motion picture on children's information, attitudes, and conduct. It is hoped that this volume will provide a necessary corrective to possible harmful results, and provide audiences for those films which sincerely and honestly convey significant interpretations of the world in which we live.

E. D.

Columbus, Ohio
September, 1933

ACKNOWLEDGMENTS

THE writer has received considerable aid from a variety of sources in the preparation of this book.

Dr. Josephine MacLatchy, Associate Editor of the *Educational Research Bulletin*, has critically edited the several experimental editions of this book and the author is indebted to her for countless constructive suggestions. Dr. W. H. Cowley, Associate Editor of the *Journal of Higher Education*, made a painstaking analysis of the material presented in the experimental edition and made many constructive suggestions for its improvement. Miss Hazel Gibbony coöperated in the preparation of the three mimeographed editions of this book, the printed experimental edition, and the present commercial edition. Mr. William Clayton Pryor aided in the preparation of the chapter on photography and made many suggestions in the selection of the illustrations for this book. Members of the National Council of Teachers of English and many other teachers used the book in their classes and made valuable suggestions for its revision. Mr. William Lewin, chairman of the Council's committee on photoplay appreciation, gave excellent coöperation.

Mr. William H. Short, Executive Director of the Motion Picture Research Council, gave many suggestions as to how to make this book a constructive factor in the development of more discriminating tastes in the field of motion pictures.

Mr. Terry Ramsaye, Editor of the *Motion Picture Herald*, made suggestions for changes in the chapter dealing with the history of the movies, and secured for us pictures of motion-picture directors. Mr. Arthur Kirk was responsible for a very pleasant visit through the Paramount studios. Mr. H. M. K. Smith made available the material dealing with costuming in motion-picture productions. Mr. Arthur DeBra of the Motion Picture Producers and Distributors of America, Inc., spent several days aiding the writer in securing satisfactory photographs. The following motion-picture producers opened their photographic files and gave assistance in securing appropriate illustrations for this book: Paramount-Publix Corporation, Metro-Goldwyn-Mayer, First National Pictures, United Artists, RKO Radio Pictures, and Principal Pictures, Inc.

The writer also wishes to express his thanks to the following authors and publishers for permission to quote from various works: to Welford Beaton for numerous quotations from the *Hollywood Spectator* and from *Know Your Movies;* to *Liberty Magazine* and to *Parents' Magazine* as sources of film ratings; to the Walt Disney Studios for material describing the making of animated cartoons; to the magazine *Time* for excerpts from articles which have appeared therein; to the *Ladies' Home Journal* for quotations from an article by Cedric Gibbons; to Iris Barry for quotations from *Let's Go to the Movies;* to Harcourt, Brace and Company for excerpts from *Principles of Literary Criticism* by I. A. Richards and *Scenario and Screen* by Frances Taylor Patterson; to Little, Brown, and Company for a quotation from *Literature in the Schools* by M. A. Dogherty; to Jonathan Cape and Harrison Smith for quotations from *The Film Till Now* by Paul Rotha; to E. P. Dutton and Company for a quotation from *Heraclitus, or The Future of Films* by Ernest Betts; and to the Chalmers Publishing Company for an excerpt from *Technique of the Photoplay* by Epes Winthrop Sargent. Complete references to all other citations will be found in the text.

TABLE OF CONTENTS

ILLUSTRATIONS

HOW TO APPRECIATE MOTION PICTURES

CHAPTER I

WHAT IS MOTION–PICTURE APPRECIATION?

Two high-school students, Bill and John, went to a movie. When they came out of the theater, Bill said, "That was a pretty ordinary picture, wasn't it?"

"Yes," John replied, "but wasn't the direction unusual?"

His friend looked a bit puzzled. "What do you mean?" he asked.

"Well, didn't you enjoy the clever way by which the director had a character back into the camera, in this way fading out the action and beginning a new type of scene in a different place on the boat?"

"I never noticed that," Bill answered.

"And didn't you like the skillful way in which the characters were introduced?" John continued. "It's the first time I have ever seen a picture in which the director introduced certain characters the way he did. You remember he had groups of persons talking about each of these characters, then the scene quickly changed to include the person about whom they were talking, and the voices of the persons commenting about him could still be heard. And didn't you notice how that one scene faded from a direct shot of the round, horn-like ventilator to the bass horn in the orchestra on a lower deck?"

"I never noticed those either," Bill replied. "But I did notice one thing which I thought was pretty good. You remember when they first showed a shot of a man shoveling food into his mouth, and then cut quickly to the engine

3

of the train and showed the fireman shoveling coal into the fire-box. Very clever, I thought. Seems strange I didn't notice the other things, though."

This little incident could be duplicated hundreds of times every day. Many persons who attend motion pictures really do not see everything that happens on the screen. They miss some of the most enjoyable parts of the picture. All they do is follow the story or plot; they pay almost no attention to the settings, to the musical accompaniment, to the clever handling of the camera, and to the skillful transition shots. And because they do not see these things, they deprive themselves of a good deal of enjoyment.

Why Study the Movies?

The purpose of this book is to help you increase your enjoyment and understanding of motion pictures. It is common, of course, for your instructors to discuss with you the appreciation of poetry, of literature, and of music, but only once in a great while do teachers try to guide students to a better appreciation of motion pictures.

In your literature classes you have learned to increase your enjoyment and understanding of the poems of Robert Frost, of Carl Sandburg, of Vachel Lindsay, of Stephen Vincent Benét, of Browning, or of Tennyson. In the field of books you have probably read with enjoyment in class and out of class the works of Robert Louis Stevenson, of Charles Dickens, of Mark Twain, of George Eliot, of Edna Ferber, of Booth Tarkington, and others. You have had courses in music appreciation in which the teacher has attempted to assist you in developing tastes for good music. In other words, you have learned not only to discover what is best in literature, music, and art, but also to prefer it.

What we are trying to do then in this book is to help you

develop standards for judging motion pictures just as your work in literature, dramatics, or music has helped you develop standards so that you can tell the difference between good and poor poems, good and poor music, good and poor drama.

But, you say, it may be true that a person needs help in learning to know the best in poetry, music, art, and drama, but one does not need any help in choosing the best in motion pictures. You may even say, "I go to the motion pictures every week and enjoy them very much." Perhaps that is true, but I am willing to make this forecast right here: Through a study of the art of the motion picture most of you will increase the enjoyment that you get from seeing motion pictures.

How can I prove the truth of what I have just said? Well, in the first place, if you read the statements of great artists or critics of art, you will see that their experiences prove that this conclusion is a sound one. For example, John Ruskin once said: ". . . the amount of pleasure that you can receive from any great work depends wholly on the quantity of attention and energy of mind you can bring to bear upon it."

Here is further proof. A large number of young people studied motion pictures as a part of their class work. They discussed standards in photography, acting, direction, and settings. They used these standards when they went to see motion pictures. And here was the result: Most of them said that through this study their enjoyment of the movies had been increased. Some persons thought that the study and analysis of motion pictures would make them distasteful to students just as some think literature teaching makes literature a bore. But the study didn't have this effect. Instead, it increased enjoyment.

Is Liking Enough?

One of the first lessons that you have to learn in developing any kind of appreciation is that liking something, just liking it, is not a satisfactory measure of its true value to you. And further, it is not a satisfactory measure of the amount of lasting enjoyment that you are going to receive. Liking something is only the first step in discovering whether it has a value for you. The next thing that you must do is to find out the consequences of indulging your wishes in this particular field. We must, then, be thoughtful about our likes and dislikes; we must understand what our likes and dislikes mean to us in the long run.

So we want you to know that through these readings and discussions we are not trying to take enjoyment away from you, but instead are trying to add understanding to it. Perhaps that is a good definition of appreciation— *to enjoy with understanding.*

The Need for Standards

To understand something is to have a measure of its worth. You cannot measure something unless you have a standard of measurement. You measure your height by a yardstick and express it in feet and inches. You measure your weight by a standard scale and get a result in pounds and ounces. And to measure the value or worth of a motion picture you must develop standards for so doing. Of course, you cannot develop standards that are as mechanical as pounds and ounces or feet and inches, but there must be standards which you can apply to the motion pictures which you view.

The group of standards presented in this book for your careful study has been found useful by other students in

judging the worth of motion pictures. Not all these standards may seem desirable to you, for standards in the appreciation of motion pictures are not the same for everyone. The standards given here, however, are more than
a group of opinions since they represent, not only the opinions of the writer, but also the ideas of many other persons.
These standards have been made in the same way that I
am asking you to make yours—by observing motion pictures, by reading what able motion-picture critics say about
them, by talking with other persons, and by trying to di-
gest what you have seen and read. I suggest that you try
these standards. Do not memorize them. If they work for
you, use them; if they do not work after a fair trial, put
them aside and try others.

Growth in appreciation comes through a willingness to
try out the standards which others have found effective.
Many persons are unwilling to do this, and they progress but
little in their tastes. Some persons go to the other extreme.
They blindly accept others' standards, but they do not make
them their own through thoughtful use. This is unwise, not
only in the enjoyment of motion pictures but in other fields
of appreciation as well.

Sometimes an overanxious teacher wants her pupils to
have what she thinks are the right tastes; she decides that
the best way to reach this happy condition is to tell students
what they ought to like and what they ought not to like.
The students, either because they do not know any better or
because they want to please their teacher, pretend that they
have the same standards. They believe that they must
agree with the teacher because it is the thing to do. Such
students will say that they enjoy a certain poem, or a certain
piece of music when it does not appeal to them at all. Such
misstatements are wholly unnecessary. Do not be a "yes

man" in matters of taste in literature, in motion pictures, in poetry. Be yourself. You must express your own judgments about motion pictures.

I am frank to confess, for example, that when motion-picture critics speak about the great skill of Charlie Chaplin and his pantomimic art, the whole discussion leaves me unmoved. I probably lack a satisfactory understanding of Chaplin's genius. Certainly, I do not believe that I am the one who is right, and that the critics are wrong. I only know that my appreciation of his art is not nearly so keen as that of many persons whose judgment in this field I respect.

On the other hand, there are some pictures which brought little acclaim from the critics, that I thought were splendid. "Michael and Mary," distributed by Universal, was one of them. "Consolation Marriage," in which Pat O'Brien and Irene Dunne starred, was another. I took keen pleasure in the direction given "Infernal Machine," and I thought that many scenes in this picture were done with rare skill.

Frankly, I must also admit that "Topaze," ranked high by many critics, left me quite unmoved and a little bored. It may be that I went expecting too much. Certainly, I did not get from it the enjoyment and insight that I had from "I Am a Fugitive from a Chain Gang," "All Quiet on the Western Front," "Arrowsmith," and other pictures.

I include these statements not to show that my opinions differ from those of other critics of motion pictures, but rather to point out that the fun of developing discriminating tastes is lost if you let some one else do your thinking for you. It is better to have tastes which others may think are inferior, but which are your own, than hypocritically to accept tastes which are considered superior when they are not really yours at all.

How Can Enjoyment Be Increased?

How can you increase your enjoyment of motion pictures? There are two ways in which this can be done. First, you can learn how to make a better selection of motion pictures. For example, when we studied the pictures that are attended by high-school students, we discovered that they do not enjoy some of the pictures which they see. If these students had read good newspaper and magazine reviews of these motion pictures, they might have stayed away from them entirely.

Not only do persons sometimes go to motion pictures which they do not enjoy, but sometimes they don't attend pictures which we are sure they would have enjoyed very much. "Cimarron," which many students rated as the best picture they had ever attended, was not seen by almost half the students in several high schools.

Try this experiment. Discover the percentage of persons in your class or club who did not see "Cimarron." You may discover, as we did, that at least half of the group did not see this picture. However, if they have seen it, I am sure that they enjoyed it intensely, because we did not find a single high-school student who disliked it. Try the same thing on "Movie Crazy," "All Quiet on the Western Front," "Disraeli," "Tom Sawyer," "Cavalcade." If you are like other groups of students who have asked themselves these questions, there are some excellent motion pictures that you did not attend, and these could have been pointed out to you at the time that they appeared. Now, this is the first way that you can increase your enjoyment— to learn how to choose the best movies and also to know which ones are poor so that you can stay away from them.

Of course, a good many of you always get some information on a picture before you go. You may ask a friend about it, or a friend may recommend a picture to you, or you may read a newspaper review of it. Many people, however, do not select with care the motion pictures that they see. Many of them just go to the movies and take a chance that the picture will be a good one.

Seeing More at the Movies

The second way in which you can increase your enjoyment is to learn to see more at the motion pictures than you now see; in other words, to get more out of the picture. In the other chapters in this book I shall discuss ways of increasing enjoyment in this fashion.

Spectators may learn to see more in the field of photography. If you watch your next motion picture carefully, you will see that the pictures have been taken with the camera at different distances and angles. Sometimes the camera is close to the object or person. This close view is used in order to direct attention to something that otherwise might not be noticed. In "Tom Sawyer," for example, we have a close-up of the pledge that Tom and Huck wrote and signed in blood.

You will also see in this picture a double exposure which is used to show Tom's thoughts. In a double exposure you see one picture right on top of the other, much like what happens when you fail to turn the film in your camera and get two pictures on one film. The double exposure is used two or three times in "Tom Sawyer." One time Tom is working in the kitchen helping his Aunt Polly put up jelly. But Tom isn't thinking about the jelly. Instead he imagines himself as a pirate on a ship, and we see a double exposure with two pictures—Tom putting up the jelly, and also Tom as a pirate.

It is always interesting, too, to see the different types of

Tom Sawyer

Is Junior Durkin well cast as Huck Finn?

Paramount

shots that directors use to introduce their characters. In "Tom Sawyer," Tom is introduced in a close-up where he is fixing the jelly glasses. Huck is later introduced in a close-up when he is imitating a cat and trying to attract Tom's attention. (See the photograph on page 11.)

CONSTRUCTIVE CRITICISM

Your group will probably be interested in discussing the ways in which motion pictures might have been improved by certain changes. For example, some time ago I saw a picture which showed a radio singer making a great success of her first broadcast. Of course one of the most important things to bring out in this successful broadcast would be the effect it had on the persons who were listening. The director of the picture was trying to show us that this girl was putting the song over to her audience in such a way as to make her a huge success. Unfortunately, however, he failed to give us enough views showing persons eagerly listening to the broadcast.

What might the director have done? One possibility would have been a picture of a miner in his rude hut listening to the broadcast and enjoying it immensely. Another might have shown a tired, overworked mother in the slum district of the city taking a brief rest and listening with enjoyment to the broadcast. We might have seen a wealthy business man in the comfort of his home, or a group of sailors lying in their bunks at sea listening to the newly discovered radio star.

In other words, the director might have given us a feeling of the great enjoyment with which people in all walks of life, high and low, rich and poor, were hearing this broadcast. He could have shown us in this way just how radio may bring great happiness to people. But he didn't do this, and I believe that his picture would have been stronger if he had. If you attended this picture, "Hello Everybody," see if you agree with me. I am certain that my enjoyment is increased by thinking about a picture in such a way.

So far, I have presented two different ways by which you can increase your enjoyment at motion pictures. First, you can use more care in selecting the motion pictures which you see. This will mean that you attend more good ones and fewer poor ones. And second, you can learn to see and hear things at the photoplay which you never saw or heard before. In other words, you can learn to appreciate the art of the motion picture.

THE EXPERIMENT

You are asked, therefore, to make an experiment in motion-picture appreciation. Throughout this book activities will be described which you are asked to try so that you may gain greater appreciation of motion pictures. Six or seven hundred students have already made this experiment. Their tastes in motion pictures were changed in some degree; they believed that the experiment was worth while; and what is more, they enjoyed it.

PROBLEMS AND ACTIVITIES

1. What does it mean when you tell a friend, "I appreciate what you have done for me?"
2. Is your appreciation of a play likely to be greater if you have acted in amateur plays? Why? Would this also be true of amateur movie making?
3. Does a painter "see" more things in a painting than one who has had no training in this art? Will he appreciate the picture more? Explain your opinion.
4. Does a person who knows a great deal about something appreciate it more than one whose knowledge in the field is not very great? Why?
5. Are your standards for selecting motion pictures which you

wish to see better now than they were when you began high school? Why?

6. Make a list of important choices—choices to do or not to do some important things—which one must make within some certain week. Do you need standards to show which is the better choice? Explain.

7. List some points which describe a "good" motion picture and those which describe a "poor" motion picture.

CHAPTER II

SHOPPING FOR YOUR MOVIES

ONE way in which you can greatly increase your enjoyment of motion pictures is to select them with greater care. In other words, you ought to shop for your movies. Now, this is not an unreasonable suggestion, is it? You shop for most things that you buy. When you go into a bookstore, you do not hand the clerk a dollar and say, "Give me a book." Instead, you have a certain book or at least a type of book in mind before you enter the store. If that kind of book is in stock, you may buy it, otherwise you go somewhere else.

How Do You Shop for Movies?

Now, why should you do any differently when you attend the theater? Certainly, it is unwise to go to a theater and buy your ticket without knowing anything about the picture. But that is exactly what you are doing, isn't it, when you go to the movies just to be doing something? How can you learn to be a good movie shopper? Well, whether a person is a good or a poor shopper depends upon how intelligently he makes his choices. What are some of the qualities of a good shopper?

In the first place, the good shopper usually looks in the newspaper to see what can be purchased and to discover prices. He does not wander aimlessly down town and buy something just because it is cheap, only to discover after he has it, that it is not at all what he wanted. The good shopper, then, knows what he needs, knows where to go to get that need satisfied, and knows a good value when he sees it.

16

Can We Depend on the "Ads"?

Certainly, we must read the announcements to discover what is being shown. Shall we accept the advertisement at its face value? If we do, we shall have to believe that every motion picture that comes to the theaters is a smashing hit, for the movie "ads" rarely suffer from a lack of modesty. Mr. W. S. Cunningham of the Columbus *Citizen* says, in the *1932 Film Daily Directors' Annual Production Guide:*

> Present-day theater advertising is the most stupendous, colossal, smashing, electrifying, greatest, sensational, wonderful, astonishing, overawing bit of exaggerated ballyhoo that has ever gagged the least discriminating of theatergoers.

So we must conclude that, while the "ads" may sometimes give some help in shopping for movies, we usually need further information. Indeed, the producers themselves are trying to keep movie advertising from giving wrong and misleading information.

Does the title of the picture tell us what it will be like? Sometimes it does, especially if it is a filming of a book or play and the name has not been changed. Occasionally, however, the producers title a picture in such a way as to give you an incorrect impression. For example, "The Admirable Crichton," when made into a movie, was titled "Male and Female." Perhaps this attracted some persons to the theater who otherwise would not have gone, but it is just as likely that it kept many persons away.

The movie "ads" do not give enough information about the picture. A much better source of information is the motion-picture reviews. Sometimes they are not well done, but if you read the reviews in the magazines and daily newspapers, you will get a great deal of help in selecting the kind of motion pictures which you enjoy.

Using the Reviews

You will find that there are certain newspaper reviewers who have tastes like your own. Sometimes you can depend fairly well upon the newspaper review as one source of evidence of whether or not a picture is likely to be an enjoyable one. But it isn't enough. Further, you cannot take time to read all the reviews because there are about five hundred motion pictures made each year. So you would have to read about two a day to pick out the good motion pictures.

Let us suppose that the picture "Cavalcade" is coming to a near-by theater next week, and you are wondering whether you wish to go. How can you find out whether it is a good picture? Of course, you can wait until some one you know sees it and then depend upon his or her report. That is a fairly satisfactory way, but sometimes you do not have friends whom you can ask, and sometimes your friends have tastes unlike your own. What can be done, then?

Magazine Reviews

Here is what I should like to suggest to you. Among the magazines which have reviews are *Time*, *Liberty*, *Parents' Magazine*, and the *Educational Screen*. These will give you a list to work from. But you need not accept a magazine rating as absolutely sound. Instead, what you may well do is to read other good reviews on any picture which you may wish to see. If you form a judgment on this basis and add to it sometimes the judgments of your friends, most of the time you will be going to better than average pictures. As a matter of fact, by careful selection you will be able to choose at least twenty-five first-class pictures to attend in a year.

How will this work out? Let us try *Liberty*, which rates

pictures in this way: one star (*), fairly good; two stars (**), good; three stars (***), excellent; four stars (****), extraordinary. As I glance down now at the three- and four-star pictures of the last six months, I see the following:

Four stars:

"Nothing Ever Happens" (a two-reel burlesque on "Grand Hotel"), "Topaze," "Rasputin and the Empress," "42nd Street," "Cavalcade," "The Animal Kingdom," "Babes in the Wood" (a Walt Disney Silly Symphony), "Silver Dollar."

Three stars:

"Reunion in Vienna," "Zoo in Budapest," "The Little Giant," "A Bedtime Story," "The Devil's Brother," "Working Man," "Hell Below," "Picture Snatcher," "Baby Face," "The Masquerader," "The White Sister," "The Rome Express," "King Kong," "The Great Jasper," "Be Mine Tonight," "The Face in the Sky," "State Fair," "Luxury Liner," "The Sign of the Cross," "She Done Him Wrong," "Grand Slam," "Tonight Is Ours," "Me and My Gal," "A Farewell to Arms," "The Son-Daughter," "If I Had a Million," "The Mummy," "The Half Naked Truth," "Three on a Match," "The Match King," "The Kid from Spain," "Cynara."

According to this reviewer, "Cavalcade" would be an excellent picture to see. I agree with this judgment, although it is my opinion that better editing of the picture would have improved it. However, I do not agree with certain of the other reports. I should not put "Topaze" in the four-star class, and I should raise "State Fair" from the three-star group to the four-star group.

As I survey this group of pictures I feel a great disappointment in the output. I will admit that there is a good deal of what might be called "entertainment value" in this group of pictures. But there is a lack of the type of picture described by one high-school girl as the kind that you doubly enjoy, first at the theater, and afterwards, thinking about them. There doesn't seem to be much to them; they have little value. There's nothing about most of them that one cares to remember. None seems to have the fundamental meaning that I discovered in "Broken Lullaby," a highly praised picture of last year. I miss here the idealism of "The Road to Life," the pathos of "The Sin of Madelon Claudet," "Arrowsmith's" story of the devotion of a scientist to his wife and to his work, the social enlightenment of "I Am a Fugitive from a Chain Gang."

The ratings I have just given you are primarily what might be called "entertainment value." We need also to have an evaluation of these pictures on something more than their entertainment value. We need to consider the social value, in other words, the effect that they are likely to have on persons who view them. Shall we look, therefore, in *Parents' Magazine* to see what they say about some of these pictures? Here are some comments from that magazine:

"Topaze." A delightfully humorous story. For Children—Beyond them. For youth—If mature, good.

"Rasputin." Drama based on the downfall of the Romanoffs. For Children—Too strong. For Youth—Very strong.

"Forty-Second Street." A back-stage drama. For Children—No. For Youth—Better not.

"Cavalcade." Moving historic panorama of family life in Great Britain. For Children—Good but heavy. For Youth—Excellent.

"Animal Kingdom, The." The successful stage play interestingly adapted to the screen. For Children—No. For Youth—Unsuitable.

"Silver Dollar." An interesting story with semi-historical background. For Children—Too mature. For Youth—Yes.

"Reunion in Vienna." Clever adaptation of Robert Sherwood's popular play. For Children and Youth—No.

"Zoo in Budapest." An unusual story of life in a zoo. For Children—Very exciting. For youth—Excellent.

"Little Giant, The." A gangster's attempts to become a gentleman of culture. For Children and Youth—Not recommended.

"Bedtime Story, A." The adventures of a gay young bachelor playing foster father to an infant. For Children—No. For Youth—Doubtful.

"Working Man, The." A charming comedy of everyday life. For Children and Youth—Yes.

"Picture Snatcher." A story of sensational pictorial journalism. For Children and Youth—No.

We see, therefore, that adult reviewers have set up another standard for these motion pictures, that of their possible harm. Some of you have seen these pictures, and perhaps nearly all of you feel that, though there may have been undesirable things in such pictures, they did not harm you. Let us suppose that they didn't. Let me ask you then this question: "Do you believe that more pictures of this type ought to be produced? Or, do you believe that there ought to be substituted for them more pictures which, like 'Cavalcade,' have not only high entertainment value, but high social value as well?" If you agree with this statement, then you must admit that your belief and your actual conduct may not be in harmony.

You Are Partly Responsible for Poor Pictures

When you attend pictures of inferior value, you are voting for their continuance, because the only way they can be continued is through sufficient returns at the box-office to justify making another one like it. "Oh well," you may say to yourself, "my little quarter doesn't make any difference. It won't make anybody rich." But when you put together the quarters of every single high-school student in the United States, what kind of total do you get? It amounts to the staggering sum of $1,100,000. So when you attend a poor picture you have voted for it just as definitely as though a ballot had been sent to you and you were given the power of deciding whether or not it ought to be produced.

Again you reply, "But there aren't enough of the pictures with high social value and high entertainment value to go 'round." You can readily see why this is so. You, and the 76,999,999 other weekly attenders of motion pictures, may not be demanding that type of picture.

A Good Shopper Knows Values

Another quality of a good shopper is that he knows values when he sees them. He is able to tell an excellent piece of goods from a poor, shoddy piece. He is able to select his purchases, not only from the standpoint of the enjoyment he will get from them, but also with their artistic qualities in mind. Now, do *you* know movie values? Can you tell a good movie from a poor one? Some of you can, but I believe that there are others who are content with third-rate pictures when they could be enjoying excellent films if only they would choose them a little more carefully.

Different Pictures for Different Moods

We go to motion pictures for different reasons at different times. Therefore we ought to select a motion picture that fits our mood. For example, one high-school girl who likes Lionel Barrymore very much went to see his picture "Sweepings." According to her statement, she went to have a lot of fun, but she discovered that "Sweepings," as she put it was "very true to life—very morbid—an old, drab thing. He died in the end. It didn't appeal to me at all."

Now this girl could have avoided her disappointment if she had taken just a few minutes to read a review of "Sweepings" before she went to the theater. A person who is in the mood for "a lot of fun" probably does not go to see a picture of this type. This must be considered in selecting a motion picture. It is true that sometimes we might be in the mood for having just a lot of good fun, see a picture that was serious, and really enjoy it, but when we wish to see something funny and light, we should keep that in mind in selecting a picture.

MAKE MOVIE-GOING A PLANNED EVENT

I believe you will find in the long run that it will be more fun to make movie-going an event, to plan on it, rather than to say, "Oh, let's go to the movies." This careless attitude is bad for two reasons: in the first place, you are likely to have a spoiled evening, and in the second place, you must remember that when you attend a poor motion picture you haven't just spoiled your evening—and that is bad enough—but you have also done something else. You have helped to pay the cost of that picture, and you have helped the producer make that kind of picture profitable.

ARE STARS ENOUGH?

Should you go to a motion picture just because your favorite star is in it? I wouldn't. But in saying this I realize that more people will probably disagree with me than will agree. It is true that one of the reasons we attend motion pictures is to see our favorite stars. But it is also true, isn't it, that if we do not pay any attention to the story or to the rest of the cast, we are likely to see our stars cast in weak stories and poorly supported by other actors and actresses? If we are careful in selecting our motion pictures, we shall select the good pictures in which our favorite stars appear. The only reason that excellent stars play in poor motion pictures is because the public supports them. If the public would refuse to see their favorites when they appear in poor pictures, we should soon have an end to excellent stars playing in a weak picture.

Substitutes for Movies

Some people go to the same theater perhaps once a week on the same night, no matter what the picture may be. It seems to me that one can spend his money a little more intelligently than this. A person ought to have enough ways of spending his spare time so that if the picture at the motion-picture theater doesn't happen to be a good one, he can use his time to good advantage in other ways.

There are at least fifty hobbies which you ought to have experimented with at some time or other during your four years in high school. You may find that out of these fifty common hobbies there are ten or fifteen which you find extremely interesting: perhaps ping pong; perhaps doing scientific experimenting; maybe staying at home and playing the radio; maybe making a collection of some kind; perhaps dancing; or whatever it may be. At any rate, you should never have to go to the motion pictures just because there is nothing else to do.

Conclusion

In conclusion, may I leave you with this one idea? By shopping for your movies you will raise the whole level of motion pictures that are produced. Poor pictures will no longer be made, and there will be many more good ones.

That seems like a great deal to result from intelligent choosing of motion pictures, doesn't it? And yet I believe the statement is a true one. So shop for your movies. By so doing you will greatly increase your leisure-time enjoyments. The rest of this book will attempt to give you a shopping guide by showing you what values may be discovered in motion pictures.

PROBLEMS AND ACTIVITIES

1. Bring to class the movie "ads" on a picture which you have seen. Were they truthful?
2. Make a study of the reviews available in daily newspapers. Which reviewers seem to agree most closely with the judgment of the class about a picture?
3. Make a list of pictures which have not only high entertainment value but high social value as well.
4. Why do we sometimes find excellent stars in poor pictures?
5. Explain to the other members of your class a type of movie substitute which you have found interesting.

CHAPTER III

THE HISTORY OF THE MOVIES

It is probably hard for young persons today to imagine a time when there were no motion pictures. Although they were invented before you were born, the movies are actually very young. I wonder if you knew that motion pictures are only about forty years old. This means, then, that when your fathers and mothers were boys and girls, they saw some of the first motion pictures that were made.

Perhaps you are interested in finding out about these early inventions, but before we discuss them, let us go back farther than the motion picture itself, and discover the steps that led up to the invention of this marvelous new instrument of communication.

Probably the earliest form of dramatic expression was story-telling. Did you ever indulge in the common habit of playing a football or basketball game all over again by describing in great detail to your friends (who may also have been there) just what happened when the fifty-yard run was made by Smith from the kick-off? "Jones kicked for South High. It was certainly a pretty kick. Smith saw it was coming to him and caught it on a dead run on the ten-yard line. Mitchell, their star tackle, came in fast, but Brown picked him off. I thought for a minute that he was going to get through, but he didn't." . . . And so the story goes on.

Why do we do it? It is primarily for the purpose of re-creating an event which once gave us a great deal of pleasure and in the repeating of which we again experience some of

26

that same thrill. An able dramatist is one who skillfully conveys to his audience certain experiences which seem important to him.

THE ORIGIN OF THE DRAMA

The history of motion pictures goes back to the earliest story-tellers. There is no doubt that in the dim days of long ago men had the same desire to retell the story of the killing of an unfriendly animal, of the fine feast attended, of the attractive girl who lived in the cave on the other side of the mountain, or of the death of a comrade. The cave-man's listeners, gathered about the fire at night, probably urged him to tell the tale again and again, especially if he were a good story-teller, and could really re-create the event for them in a dramatic way.

Perhaps in the first telling a single person dramatized the event as well as he could without any assistance. Later, the number of players increased, and from this practice developed our modern theater. This was a crude beginning, of course, this telling of a story in which more than one person participated and in which the characters of the piece were taken by different individuals.

The drawing of crude pictures was another step in the representation of reality, although some time was to elapse before they were to supplement or to supplant the drama. The pictures were, of course, easy to understand, and in the beginning must have been highly satisfactory. But they had one major difficulty: they did not move; they could only suggest motion.

The development of the puppet show was an attempt to make possible a more accurate portrayal of certain types of characters—a portrayal in which motion played an important part. But again the puppets were not so real as desired. They were only makeshifts for reality, satisfactory, doubtless, in the same sense that dolls are satisfactory to children, but not entirely satisfactory as a method of truly re-creating an event.

Early Developments in the Motion Picture

How drawings could be made to move was a question which probably bothered a good many persons. One solution to the problem is a method which you probably have used yourself. Did you ever draw little pictures similar to each other, near the edge of the successive sheets of your writing tablet? Each picture was just a little different from the one before; that is, if you were making a picture of a man walking, you would put his legs in slightly advanced positions in each successive picture. Then, when you had finished drawing these pictures at the edge of the tablet, you flicked the edges with your thumb, and the man seemed to be walking.

This idea was used in what was perhaps the first practical idea of a motion-picture machine. The device was called "The Wheel of Life" and appeared in England in 1833. It was a hollow cylinder with drawings inside and slits in the upper part of the cylinder through which the observer looked. When the cylinder was rotated, the object in the pictures, usually a horse or a dancer, seemed to be moving. This, you see, was similar to the device that many school children have used.

The reason these pictures seem to be moving is because after looking at an object an impression, called an afterimage, continues in the eye; that is, the image of what you have observed persists for a short time after you have looked at the object, and it merges with the next image. In the motion-picture camera it has been discovered that if these little pictures on the screen change every one-sixteenth of a second, it is sufficient to cause the feeling that the picture is moving.

"The Wheel of Life" was followed by a number of other inventions of a similar nature. The machines had such curious names as "autoscope," "motorscope," "vibroscope," and "zoetrope." All of these, you must remember, were toys, and were not thought of as commercial possibilities in the sense that the motion picture of today is.

After moving figures or photographs became a reality, it remained only to improve the process. In 1860 Coleman Sellers, a mechanical engineer, made a device which was still closer to the present motion-picture projector. He first took photographs of his sons in a series of actions showing them driving a nail into a box. He then put these photographs on the blades of a paddle wheel which could be revolved. When a person looked at these revolving blades, he saw the boys in action, pounding the nail into the box. But there was one difficulty with this method; it did not give the image a period of rest, as does the motion-picture projector.

The next development in motion pictures grew out of a conversation and a difference of opinion among a group of horsemen in California. Some argued that a racing horse had all four feet off the ground at the same moment. Others said that this notion was absurd and that a racing horse never had all his feet off the ground at the same time. This incident took place in 1872 on the ranch of Leland Stanford, the founder of Leland Stanford University. Mr. Stanford decided that the argument could be settled by having a series of photographs (not motion pictures, of course, just ordinary snapshots) taken of a racing horse as he moved along the track. John D. Isaacs, an engineer, then devised for Stanford a battery of cameras with electrical shutter controls. One of the men interested in the argument was Edward Muybridge, a skilled photographer, who was engaged in making surveys for the United States government. Muybridge operated the twenty-four cameras at the edge of the race course. These cameras were controlled by electrical wire contacts in the track which were operated by the tires of the sulky drawn by the racing horse. It was discovered that the horse was entirely off the ground at certain times.

Further Improvements

According to Terry Ramsaye, who wrote a fascinating history of the motion picture,[1] Edison's desire to give eyes to his phonograph is primarily responsible for the present motion-picture camera. Having perfected his "talking machine," Edison wished to have this phonograph tied up with pictures. Even though he abandoned his efforts along these lines for a time, he was destined to make the next contribution to motion-picture development.

Edison's first pictures were recorded in spirals upon a cylinder, somewhat like the early phonograph record. But what was needed was some sort of flexible, continuous film upon which pictures could be taken. Edison was assisted in solving this problem by George Eastman, the founder of the now well-known Eastman Kodak Company. Eastman had put upon the market a flexible film that was wound up on a spool and which could be exposed as desired. Edison obtained some of this new film and used it successfully in his new motion-picture machine.

He called his invention a "kinetoscope" and demonstrated it in his laboratories at West Orange, New Jersey, in the year 1889. He kept on experimenting until at last it was possible to look through the peephole of the machine and see a series

[1] Ramsaye, Terry, *A Million and One Nights*, New York: Simon and Schuster, 1926.

of pictures, about fifty feet in total length, showing a person in movement. They were jerky and interrupted pictures, but they did move! It is said that the first moving picture taken was one of a sneeze, performed by an assistant in the laboratory, Mr. Fred Ott. This sneeze was the subject of the first film to be offered to the public. Other Edison productions at this time included a troop of trained bears, some performing dogs, cats, and monkeys, a solo dance, a contortionist, a strong man, and a small bit from a popular stage success.

This kinetoscope was a one-man show, just as the stereoscope which you may have seen in your grandmother's parlor can be used by only one spectator at a time. The kinetoscope was patented by Edison in 1891, and it was first publicly shown at a kinetoscope parlor in New York, April 14, 1894. The fact that only one person could watch the picture at a time was a real handicap, and another weakness was the impossibility of handling more than fifty feet of film at a time. But, interestingly enough, Edison had discouraged efforts to develop a projector which would make it possible for a great many persons to see at the same time, because he said that it would cause the novelty of the motion picture to wear off too quickly. He looked on the motion picture as a toy, not even suspecting that it was to become as basic an art as that of printing.

Meanwhile, other experimenters were active in Europe, all aiming at a combination of the kinetoscope with the magic lantern. In 1895, a year later than Edison's exhibition, a man named Woodville Latham gave public demonstrations in America of a projector using the kinetoscope film pictures, but the process was crude and unsuccessful. The Latham brothers originated also a simple device known as the "Latham Loop" which left a piece of slack film between the two sprockets and the main body of the film, in this way removing the strain which had previously caused the film to break.

The principle upon which the modern projector is based, however, is that of Thomas Armat's machine, which was shown publicly for the first time at the Cotton States' Exposition, in Atlanta, Georgia, in September, 1895. Armat's vitascope, which was incorrectly coupled with Edison's name for box-office reasons, was then shown on Broadway and was an immediate success. But the progress of motion pictures in America was slowed down by a number of lawsuits over patents. Further, this form of entertainment received a serious set-back abroad when at Paris in 1897 a disastrous fire in a motion-picture theater took the lives of 180 members of Parisian society.

EARLY MOTION PICTURES

The fifty-foot lengths of film used in the kinetoscope lengthened until in 1897 eleven thousand feet of film were shown, a motion-picture record of the Corbett-Fitzsimmons fight at Carson City, Nevada. During the same year a film version, about three thousand feet long, of the Oberammergau Passion Play was made by Richard Hollaman. This was not filmed abroad, as its title would indicate, but was made in this country.

In 1903, however, Edwin S. Porter, an Edison cameraman, tried to introduce some new ideas into the field of motion pictures, interest in which was declining. He produced two pictures which have given us the pattern for a certain type of American motion picture. They were "The Life of an American Fireman" and "The Great Train Robbery." These were successful, and were followed by other films of this type.

One- or two-reel pictures were the common fare up to about 1912. In 1913 an eight-reel picture, "Quo Vadis," was produced in Italy and was unusually successful. From 1911 to 1914 the industry developed with astounding rapidity. But the most sensational pictures were coming from Europe, and had considerable influence on the American producers.

With the outbreak of the war in 1914, film production in Europe came to an end. And at this time America obtained the commercial control of motion pictures, a control which she still holds. America's output increased yearly throughout the war period, until 1918 found her completely controlling the world market. At the present time, Hollywood, California, is the film center of the United States. How long it will continue to remain so, no one knows. In the past, some films have been made in the East and it is possible that in the future New York City will loom larger as a production center.

With the next great development—sound—we come into a period which you know quite well. Interestingly enough, we had talking pictures much earlier than 1926, as this clipping from the Columbus *Citizen* of May 31, 1908, shows:

Keith's [theater] will open Sunday for summer bookings of motion pictures. On Monday, the wonder of the age, the cameraphone, will begin producing talking pictures.

These will be a novelty and Keith's has the exclusive right for them in Columbus. As the pictures on the screen move, the characters will speak by means of a phônographic arrangement.

They give a most realistic reproduction of the Georgia Minstrels and the act of the vaudeville stars, Ford and Emmett.

In addition to the talking pictures, regular moving pictures and illustrated songs will be on the program. Prices 5 and 10 cents. Shows, 1:30 p. m. to 5; 7 to 10:30 p. m.

When sound was finally successfully linked with motion pictures in 1926, there was a good deal of criticism, especially among the motion-picture critics, of the new talking picture. They said that it violated screen art, that to introduce sound was inartistic. Many said that the new medium was only a fad and would soon be a thing of the past. Some critics were even so rash as to predict the length of time that it would take before the new plaything was cast aside.

But all those who predicted that sound and talking pictures would soon give way to the old silent pictures have not yet proved their skill at prophesying. It is true that there is less dialogue in pictures today than there was in 1927 and that the dialogue now included is greatly improved, but, as far as I can see, there is little or no demand for a return of silent pictures. We still have these sound and talking motion pictures, and no one knows what the future holds for the industry. In 1930, from fifty million to seventy-five million people in the United States viewed the motion pictures every week. In twenty-five years the motion picture has almost completely changed the recreational habits of the American people.

Future Inventions

What may be ahead of us in the way of inventions? The dream of the inventors is three-dimension motion pictures to replace our two-dimension pictures. You would then see pictures like those which you see when looking through a stereoscope. There have also been experiments with screens much wider than the present ones. But whatever experiments are made, whatever ingenious new inventions are added to the motion picture, we can be quite certain that, at least for the next twenty-five years. the motion picture will represent one of the most widespread leisure-time activities of the great mass of American people.

MORE ABOUT OUR EXPERIMENT

The motion picture is a machine and, like all machines, has no purpose; it is merely a tool to be used by persons who supply the purpose. Machines in themselves are neither good nor bad. The purpose of this book is to help you see that the purpose back of motion-picture production should be social. Every individual has a job in connection with that program, and one of the important parts of that job is to be intelligent about the motion picture and what it can do. Every year our motion-picture studios turn out five hundred or more full-length motion pictures in addition to comedies, newsreels, and short-length pictures. We need to consider the effect of these pictures on American life. These movies must be evaluated.

The swiftness of the appearance of the motion picture has made it hitherto impossible for teachers, parents, or others systematically to aid youth in the proper selection and evaluation of motion pictures, but the time is now ripe for it. We have, therefore, arranged for you in this book a series of readings and projects which we hope will enable you to make more intelligent selections of motion pictures and to gain an understanding of the rôle they should play in our modern world.

PROBLEMS AND ACTIVITIES

1. Did you ever think about the funny papers as telling stories through motion pictures? How is it done? By dialogue? By suggesting motion?
2. Discuss the relationship between the interest in the funny papers and the movie comedies. Do the comic strips suggest motion? How?

3. How might television affect our recreational habits?
4. Do you think that you can really do anything to direct the course of motion pictures into a more satisfactory channel? If so, how?
5. Write a review of a current picture.
6. Take the Thurstone test of motion-picture attitude to see what your group thinks of motion pictures. (It can be purchased from the University of Chicago Press.)

CHAPTER IV

A VISIT TO A STUDIO

PROBLEMS IN MOTION-PICTURE PRODUCTION

THE job of producing a motion picture is even more complicated than that of writing a novel or a drama, or staging a play. First, there must be a written story which the camera will change from words into pictures. It is true, of course, that words do now play a part in motion pictures, but it is possible to produce good motion pictures with few or no words. One cannot, however, have motion pictures without pictures. So, when the story is changed into a scenario, the director still has a number of problems—working with the art director; coöperating with the costume director; obtaining proper locations, satisfactory motion-picture equipment, an adequate cast, and competent cameramen; and being able to assemble the motion picture skillfully once it has been filmed.

The production of a satisfactory motion picture is a difficult task, and because of its difficulty, such an achievement deserves great praise. Indeed, one of the reasons why we have so few good motion pictures is because we have so few truly capable writers, directors, art directors, and actors. The uncertainty of getting an author's thoughts on the screen satisfactorily was illustrated by Dreiser's great disappointment with the film version of *An American Tragedy*, while Sinclair Lewis thought that a splendid job had been done with *Arrowsmith*.

In order to give you some understanding of the making of motion pictures, let me describe to you a visit to the studios of one of the major producers. We first interviewed the persons responsible for making motion pictures, and then we were taken to see the pictures being filmed. Throughout our visit we were fortunate to be accompanied by the art director of the studio. In reply to our question about the form in which the story of the motion picture first comes to the studio, the director said that when the story reaches the studio its sequences have already been decided. The form in which it appears is called the "working script." In this script are found the various specifications for buildings, not entirely complete, of course, but in sufficient detail for the men in the studio to obtain a general idea of what sets are required.

The script may call for unusual or little known scenes and costumes. In that case, the members of the research department are asked to obtain photographs and information regarding these topics. For example, if the picture under production deals with China, they know with some degree of certainty the type of scenes desired. They will, however, wish to be sure that their ideas are accurate, so the head of the research department will be requested to search his files and to take out all material dealing with the specific type of Chinese dwellings and costumes needed in the play.

If he finds that his library does not have enough information on these subjects, he will go to the larger libraries, make a list of the photographs in books which he wishes to have copied, and arrange to have the copies made. When the research work is finished—and it must be completed by a certain date—the various photographs are used in the planning of the sets.

AN AËRIAL VIEW OF THE METRO-GOLDWYN-MAYER STUDIOS

This general view of a studio shows that everything is not as real as it seems.

Settings

The art director then consults with the director of the picture and draws up specifications for the various sets. These are sometimes reproduced in miniature in cardboard so that a satisfactory idea of what the final sets will look like may be obtained. All such sets are, of course, worked out to scale so that the persons in charge can determine easily whether or not certain types of shots which they want will be secured. Since the space in a studio is limited, and since sets for several pictures are being prepared at the same time, the executive in charge of production must be certain that there is adequate room for all the types of shots which are desired.

When these sets have been approved by the director and his staff, plans for the building of the sets are then drawn up in the same way that an architect draws such plans. There is, however, one important difference. An architect usually plans a building for some one to live in or work in; the motion-picture draftsman plans his structure so that it can be photographed satisfactorily. His sets must always be designed for the action which will take place on them. He must make certain that the cameras can be placed in the position necessary to secure the desired shots. When these plans are finally approved, a building program is worked out. Cedric Gibbons, art director of Metro-Goldwyn-Mayer, said in a recent article that forty sets was the average required for each of their feature pictures. Since space in the studio is at a premium, the sets must be put up with all possible speed.

Length of Time Required for Production

Our next question was, How long does it take to make a picture? We learned that the production schedule runs from eighteen to twenty-one days. The persons concerned sometimes work day and night to rush the picture to completion in order to use the space for the next production. Special productions often take longer than three weeks, however.

Our trip was interrupted every now and then by the ringing of a gong. This meant that the shooting of a picture was on and that everyone must be silent. Since nearly all the motion pictures made in studios today are sound pictures, and since the microphones are very sensitive, everyone in the huge studio must be quiet when a scene is being filmed or strange and undesired noises may be picked up.

One of the first sets we saw was one showing a wealthy mandarin's garden. It resembled in remarkable degree a photograph which the art director had previously shown us. Even at close range, it was difficult to discover that the grass was not genuine.

Long Rehearsals

While we were there, we saw the rehearsal of a scene for a picture which was being made. It took a long time to adjust the lights on the scene. Several times a group of Chinese servants was asked to hurry through a door and show surprise when they found their master dead on the floor. After many rehearsals the cameraman was told to get ready, and the action was finally shot. Since the director was satisfied with the picture, no retake was ordered.

We saw another scene from the same picture. A policeman entered and quizzed the persons who were in the room. This scene was rehearsed at least ten times before the director was satisfied with it. (If the average feature picture runs for seventy minutes at the theater, and it takes twenty-one days to make it, each working day then accounts for an average of three and a half minutes of usable film.)

SHANGHAI EXPRESS

Paramount

This picture was not taken in Shanghai, as may be seen from the photograph. In the film, however, the illusion of reality was highly satisfactory.

Reality of Settings

In the course of our visit we went outside where we saw, a few hundred feet away, what appeared to be a large Spanish dwelling built of brick. I wondered whether it was really made of brick, so I inquired of the art director whether many of the sets were faked. He replied that if they were, it would simplify matters a great deal, but he assured us that we should see shortly that some of the buildings were very substantial. He said that the brick building was constructed like any other brick building. Of course, it was only a front, since that was all which was needed in the scene. He assured us that many sets are not the flimsy structures which people commonly imagine them to be.

In another set a courtroom was being built. The head of the research department had spent several days getting specifications from the county courthouse in a neighboring city, and it was being reproduced in almost complete detail. The set, except that it lacked a roof, was an almost exact duplicate of the courthouse.

Standards for Judging Sets

We asked the art director for suggestions as to the standards which a spectator ought to apply to the sets of a motion picture, and how to evaluate the sets used. He said that there was one simple, but good, rule for such an evaluation; the set ought to duplicate, as far as possible, the circumstances or surroundings under which the event to be photographed took place. If the script calls for a Chinese home, the set ought to look like such a home. Also, there should be sufficient atmosphere really to establish the setting of a picture. He showed us a set which duplicated one end of a large steamer. He said that by first taking a long shot of the original steamboat in the water and by alternating it with closer shots of this set, the observer of the picture truly sensed the atmosphere of the sea and was not conscious that the picture was made in a studio. Such practices as this lend the illusion which one experiences when he sees a moving picture. If the spectator does not fall under the spell of the illusion, the failure is due in part, at least, to poor and unsuitable sets.

Costuming

One of the important factors in developing the reality and proper atmosphere of the play is the costuming. In order to discover the relationship of proper costuming to the development of good motion pictures, we interviewed Mr. H. M. K. Smith, who for a long time was costume director for Famous-Players-Lasky. We asked him the same kind of questions that we had put to the art director at the other studio, and in reply to the question, "What are the standards by which you judge the costuming in a picture?" he said that a character in a play must dress the part that is called for in the story, an actress should sacrifice her own personality to that of the character she is impersonating. This may sometimes mean that she will not appear beautiful on the screen. But when the script calls for a shabby, poverty-stricken character, then the costuming should bring out that idea skillfully. It is not always easy to accomplish this. One time a famous star who was to act the part of a factory worker in one of the Lasky pictures had the dress for these scenes made of a most expensive material at one of the highest priced establishments on Fifth Avenue. The cost of that factory girl's dress was $485. Needless to say, it looked silly on the screen.

We asked Mr. Smith whether or not expensive materials could be faked satisfactorily. He said that through bitter

CIMARRON

Note the great amount of detail to insure accuracy in the clothing and hairdress of these characters.

experience they had found that, if the girl in the story is rich and lives in luxury, the actress usually cannot dress in cheap fabrics even though they photograph satisfactorily, because wearing faked things reacts unfavorably upon the actress's performance.   She must be wearing real silks and satins. Faked stuff will not do.

We inquired whether attention had to be paid to colors of garments, and we were told that certain colors photograph better than others.   However, if the whole cast dressed in black, white, and gray—all colors which photograph well— their actions would lose color and variety.   Directors try to see, therefore, that the women are dressed in clothes which not only photograph well, but which have the desired mental effect upon them.

We asked then: "Do you believe that the clothing shown in the average motion picture is satisfactory both from the standpoint of photography and from the standpoint of accuracy?" Mr. Smith replied:

No, the age of common sense has not yet been reached.   I saw one picture in which there were four butlers in a single house, and the parlor and personal maids of the movies, with their four-inch heels and chiffon hose visible far above the knee, would not be tolerated by employers either in this country or abroad.   I once had a heated argument with a famous director who demanded six tea wagons with a sextette of identically dressed maids to wheel them about at a very smart tea at the house of a social leader.

Furthermore, it would be most unwise for any American to copy her wardrobe after that of the motion-picture star.   In spite of the advice of the costume director, these ladies of the screen often insist on wearing the wrong clothes.   One production which dated back to the time of the first railroads in America presented the heroine in a tight-fitting cloche hat not three weeks out of Paris.   In another picture all the nuns wore high French heels and sheer silk hose.

Only in rare cases can the technical staff be blamed for these errors. As a rule the technical staff consists of intelligent and earnest men and women who spend long hours in research, rush about with books of etiquette, and with historical and scientific volumes make a complete technical analysis and guide for the director's use. Then they sit back and weep when they see the final product on the screen because it has departed so far from what they know is accurate.

Developing, Printing, and Editing the Film

From this visit to the studio we learned that these steps are followed in the making of a picture:

1. The selection of a story.
2. The construction of a scenario.
3. The selection of a director, art director, and cast.
4. The erection of sets and selection of locations.
5. The photographing of the story according to the scenario.
6. Assembling the film in final form.

As shooting goes on, the film is sent to the laboratories for ' development and printing. In this way the director of a picture knows which scenes have been satisfactorily photographed and which need to be retaken.

When the whole picture has been photographed according to the scenario, then the film editor faces the task of assembling it in the final form. He may decide to arrange the scenes in a way different from that called for in the scenario. He will be aided in his decisions by the judgments of other technical men and by showings to preview audiences. A scene that was intended to be sad may seem funny to the preview audience. It will either have to be taken out, or the scene will have to be photographed again. Some part may go over especially well, and the editor may decide to increase the emphasis on this part of the film. When it is finally ready, he sends it to the laboratory, where from eighty to

THREE LITTLE PIGS   *United Artists*

The animated cartoon offers a medium for the portrayal of fairy tale and
fantasy. The ideas it presents are limited only by the imagination of the artist.

two hundred fifty duplicates, called "positives," are made.
These positives are then rushed to the various first-run
theaters in the country, where the public will decide their
fate.

THE MAKING OF ANIMATED CARTOONS

We have discussed at length the making of regular feature
motion pictures. Would you be interested in visiting a
studio which has no sets, no paid actors, a studio whose
assets are the creative minds of the artists plus plenty of ink,
drawing pens, and cameras? Shall we drop in at the Walt
Disney Studios, which in 1933 will produce twenty-six cartoons, thirteen of which will be Mickey Mouse, and thirteen
Silly Symphonies in Technicolor? Perhaps you have seen
"Babes in the Wood" and "Three Little Pigs," which have
just appeared.

The first question that you will wish to ask the guide
about these cartoons is, Where do you get your stories?
Does one man actually furnish all the ideas? The guide will
tell you that the Story Department is one of their most
important divisions, and that the first step in production is a
rough draft of the story that is to be filmed. Here, for example, is a tentative story outline for "Santa's Workshop":

United Artists Symphony No. 7, *Santa's Workshop;* Jackson, *Director;* Churchill, *Musician.*

Story opens showing exterior of Santa's workshop at the
North Pole—beautiful scene, snow falling, etc., Santa's factory buildings.

Dissolve into an exterior of Santa's stables; little gnomes busily
grooming the reindeer, washing their teeth, etc.; all busy and
whistling, or some other musical effect.

This dissolves to the interior of the workshop, showing happy
gnomes busily operating the quaint machinery; all gnomes
whistle as they work. Show various closeups of individual elves

making toys. Everything is run in the manner of the Ford factory. (Plenty of opportunities here for showing the ludicrous methods used by the gnomes in making the toys.)

Santa is the big boss who "okays" all the toys. He is happy and very good natured, and gets a big kick out of the various things the toys do. Santa could teach the dolls to speak and say "mama."

Amusing action of toys of various kinds, walking in their own individual ways. The toy band strikes up a snappy march and all join in a big procession leading to Santa's bag. When all the toys enter the bag, Santa picks it up, puts it into his sleigh, and drives off. Make a beautiful final scene, Santa disappearing in the sky in the distance, all the elves singing a Christmas song; just before the iris closes, show a silhouette effect of his reindeer and sleigh as they cross the Christmas moon, the voices of the elves coming in full volume for a final finish effect on the end title.

Everyone think this over and have some good "gags" ready to hand in at the next gag meeting. I expect a big turnout on this story.

Walt

An outline such as this is prepared for each picture and distributed to the staff at a meeting held to arrange plans for pictures. The story is discussed, and the men later hand in their suggestions for "gags" and situations. The Story Department then prepares a scenario for the picture, and another conference is held with the director and the musician. The "set designer" or "layout man" is included in this conference since it is his job to prepare rough sketches of the complete scenes, from which the background sketches are drawn up. These are the stage settings for the action, and the portions of the scene which will be occupied by the animated figures must be left clear.

The action and the musical accompaniment are worked out by the director and the musician in great detail, and are then given to the "animators," the men who do the actual

drawing. Inasmuch as 10,000 to 15,000 individual drawings are required for one cartoon feature, the story has to
be broken down into several scenes and these scenes are
distributed among many animators. This means that the
various men must adopt a standard style of drawing—sometimes a difficult task. The company trains its own animators.
During the apprenticeship period, which lasts at least six
months, the apprentice is required to attend art classes at
the studio.

Each animator is given detailed instructions by the director as to the nature of the scene, the exact footage, the
tempo of the musical accompaniment, and the scene's relationship to the picture as a whole. He is also given the
background sketch, and is then supposed to make a series
of progressive drawings of the scene. These he numbers
serially, in the order in which they are to be photographed.
The size of these drawings is approximately seven by nine
inches. Each animator has an assistant and usually two
apprentices to help him. In order to save time, the animator
himself makes drawings of only the extreme action, and his
assistant fills in the intervening drawings, which are then
turned over to the apprentices, who add all the necessary
detail.

When the scene is completed, the drawings are sent to
the Inking and Painting Department where the drawings are
traced with black India ink on sheets of celluloid, the same
size as the paper. As soon as the tracing has dried, the
celluloid sheet is turned over, and the area occupied by the
figures on the drawing is painted over. This is done so that
the background will not show through them. A single background is used for each scene, and the action occurring
against this background is shown by the figures painted on
the celluloid sheets, which are placed over the background.

Thus, by placing these sheets of celluloid on top of each other, all stacked on top of the same background, it is possible to show a large number of characters, each doing something different. The camera is usually placed above the picture with the lens pointed directly toward the floor. Each picture, therefore, is inserted below the camera and photographed in this way.

A single cartoon averages about 600 feet of film, and an animator takes at least eight hours to draw the pictures for 5 feet of action. Approximately 100 hours are required to photograph these 600 feet, and if there should be a number of "trick" shots the shooting may take as long as 125 or even 150 hours.

While the picture is being animated, inked, and photographed, the sound record is being made. Since the musical score has been prepared with the same tempos as those used in drawing the picture, and the musical director knows the exact spot in the picture where each musical note or sound effect will occur, it is not necessary even to see the picture in order to score it. An orchestra, ranging from twelve to twenty members, and four or five men for producing sound effects, are used. In order to synchronize the sound perfectly, the conductor and each member of the orchestra wear headphones through which they hear the exact beat of the music to be played.

The animated cartoon must of course be judged by different standards from those of the regular feature picture. No one expects them to show real life. They deal with fantasy, fairy tales, the highly imaginative adventures of imaginary persons, animals, or objects.

Producers of Motion Pictures

A student of motion pictures should be familiar with the names of the film producers. Although one cannot forecast exactly the type of picture that each organization makes, nevertheless there is a tendency for them to be associated with certain types of pictures. The names of the important producing organizations, therefore, are listed here:

1. Columbia Pictures Corp.
2. First National Productions
3. Fox Film Corp.
4. Metro-Goldwyn-Mayer
5. Paramount Publix Corp.
6. RKO Pathe-RKO Radio Pictures
7. United Artists Corp.
8. Universal Pictures Corp.
9. Warner Bros. Pictures
10. World Wide Pictures

I should like to be able to tell you that certain of these organizations produce pictures that are always satisfactory. However, I cannot do this because good and poor pictures are produced by each of these companies. For example, "All Quiet on the Western Front" was produced by Universal, "Arrowsmith" was produced by United Artists, Paramount put out "Broken Lullaby," and Warner Bros. was responsible for "Disraeli." All of these were superior films.

Do not forget that many excellent films have been imported from foreign countries. Among them are: "Two Hearts in Three-Fourths Time," "Variety," "The Cabinet of Dr. Caligari," "The Last Laugh," "Under the Roofs of Paris," "Siegfried," "The Road to Life," and "The Red Head."

PROBLEMS AND ACTIVITIES

1. Why are most motion pictures now made at Hollywood?
2. How can the public help to prevent bad taste in costuming?
3. How can one best get the writer, who has the meaning, and

the director, who has the means, together? Is there hope of developing writers who are directors as well?

4. What "boners" have you noticed in motion pictures?
5. Report to the class on some of the activities at a motion-picture studio. (Consult the sources mentioned at the back of this book.)
6. Find out the number of feature pictures made last year by each of the major producers. Do you think that we would have much better pictures if each of these companies cut their production schedule in half? Why?

CHAPTER V

MOTION–PICTURE REVIEWING

A MOTION-PICTURE review is a criticism, a statement of the strong and weak points of a picture. There are various kinds of reviews, and there are a number of purposes that one may have in reviewing a picture. You may review a picture orally. For example, you may say to your friend, "You ought to see 'Eskimo.' It has some striking shots of scenes in the Arctic." This is a kind of review, and points out that the scenes or settings of the picture provide one of the enjoyable features.

There are also written reviews of motion pictures. These usually are done by persons specially trained to write them. The daily newspapers and the weekly and monthly magazines have motion-picture critics who write reviews. Some of you may have occasion to write newspaper reviews. Certainly, you have an opportunity to write these reviews for your high-school paper. Others of you may be able to do some reviewing for your local newspapers.

How does one review a motion picture? In the first place, to do a satisfactory piece of reviewing, you ought to sit through two viewings of the film. The first viewing will acquaint you with the main details of the picture. The second time, you will be able to watch carefully for skill in direction, acting, and so on. If we study reviews, we see that the writer is setting up certain standards for motion pictures. He sets up standards for the photography, the story, the acting, the direction, the lighting, the dialogue, and sound. You can see this by the following extracts from motion-picture reviews.

The Story

The motion-picture review usually gives some notion of the story, so that you can determine whether it is the type of picture that you wish to see. Here is an example—a review of "Cavalcade" by Irene Thirer in the New York *Daily News:*

Noel Coward's story has to do with the Marryot family of London and their servants down-stairs. The locale at start is 1899—Boer War time. Robert Marryot is about to forsake his charming wife and two small sons to fight the war in Africa.

Down-stairs, Alf, the butler, is packing his bag, despite the tears of his wife Ellen, the maid. He, too, will leave his family behind. . . . But British women must be brave. And, eventually, the war is over, and both the master and the butler return safe and sound.

The years elapse. Alfred, who had been a loving husband, has bought a public house and drinks the profits. He is cruel to his wife and vicious to his little daughter, fast becoming accomplished in the art of dancing. And he meets death at the hoofs of a team of runaway horses turning the curb near his pub.

More years elapse. Marryot is Sir Robert now—knighted for his gallantry in the Boer War. His son Edward marries a lovely girl who had been his childhood chum. They honeymoon— on the Titanic. And more years pass. It is 1914. Father and younger son now fight for England in the World War. And mother must be brave. Sir Robert comes out of it safely, but ironically enough the news of Joie's death is received by his grief-stricken mother on the very day of the Armistice when Ellen, now the snooty Mrs. Bridges, is visiting and telling Lady Marryot that her daughter, to-day a famous actress and really beloved of the deceased Joie, is quite good enough for the Marryot scion.

ESKIMO

Metro-Goldwyn-Mayer

The motion picture is especially valuable in giving us documentary records of how people live.

After you read this account of the story you see at once that it is not a comedy. It is a picture like "Cimarron" or "The Covered Wagon" or "A Tale of Two Cities." You know in general what to expect.

Direction

The reviewer may also comment on *direction*, as does Welford Beaton in his review of "Mata Hari":

> In his script George Fitzmaurice, the director, had a better story than von Sternberg had when he directed Marlene Dietrich in "Dishonored," which had the same central character. But what a difference between the pictures! The von Sternberg offering bristled with inspired directorial touches; Fitzmaurice's is devoid of a single instance of brilliant direction. Fitz gives us actors speaking lines; von Sternberg gave us people speaking their thoughts. "Mata Hari" is dull solely because it was given dull direction. Fitz had everything out of which a really notable picture could have been made, but he brings it down to ordinary program level by his failure to realize its possibilities for something higher.

In Chapter XI we shall give you a good deal more information as to what these directorial touches are, and we shall offer some standards which may be used in rating the direction of a picture.

The Truth of the Story

Here is another review, by Dalton Trumbo, in the *Hollywood Spectator:*

> The weakness of "Homicide Squad" seems to be a weakness of story—a complete denial of all probabilities in an effort to keep things in high gear from start to finish. For some time I have longed to pick one of these gangster affairs to pieces so far as logic is involved, and that I finally yield to the temptation does not denote that the present picture is either better or worse than a dozen that have gone before.

Item one: George Brent, son of the chief of the homicide squad, is sent as a spy to the gang headquarters, the idea being that nobody will know who he is. Is that peculiar, or am I just a meanie? *Item two:* Recognized as a police spy, he is murdered in Carrillo's rendezvous, and no effort is made to conceal his body or to move it elsewhere. *Item three:* Carrillo is surprised in a basement by three officers armed with machine guns. All three open fire, and with bullets pouring at the rate of twenty or thirty a second from a distance of less than twenty feet, Carrillo escapes unhurt to an adjoining room. *Item four:* He then replies in kind through a six inch square peep hole. A bullet entering the peep hole would kill him, yet those machine guns simply can't hit the target. *Item five:* The story ends with the gangster chief's death, and with not a shred of evidence against the remainder of his cronies. The gang still remains. *Item six:* The gangsters speak of being "put on the spot," which, if I am up on my gangsters, went out of use in the best circles some eighteen months ago.

The reviewer is referring, of course, to the common habit of exaggeration in motion pictures and the use of stories which could by no chance be probable. I am sure that Mr. Trumbo would be the last one to maintain that every single item which went into the picture must have once occurred. However, there is no reason why pictures cannot be made probable. Improbability in a picture is usually caused by carelessness in construction. But should all pictures be true to life? What about comedies, fantasies, burlesques, farces? We shall talk about this in much greater detail in Chapter XII.

ACTING

An example of a reviewer's criticism of the acting in a motion picture is the following excerpt from William S. Cunningham's review of "Broken Lullaby," in the Columbus *Citizen:*

BROKEN LULLABY   *Paramount*

Able critics named this film one of the best pictures of 1932. Note the careful attention that is given to detail. What is the man on the roof doing?

Lionel Barrymore, as the German father, gives a superb performance. At all times he is the complete master of the situation. His one scene in the German saloon where he orders "one beer" then rebukes his life-long friends for their hatred of the French, is the dramatic highlight of the film, a scene which will grip you as few scenes have done. It is splendid acting—and a powerful argument against war as is, for that matter, the entire story.

Photography

A discussion of the skill in photography displayed in this same picture is given in the magazine *Time:*

The creative skill which used to show in the smooth touches which Lubitsch put into his comedies comes out here in other directions—a shot of marching feet for which the camera was placed just behind a one-legged soldier; doorbells ringing in the Falsburg shops as the shopkeepers come out to watch a Frenchman going down the street; a grave-digger telling the German boy's fiancée (Nancy Carroll) that a Frenchman stopped to speak to him and gave him a tip.

Settings

You may also be interested in the following excerpt from a review of "State Fair" which appeared in the *Nation:*

The most important thing about "State Fair" . . . is that it marks a possible tendency of the same sort in the films. Not since Wallace Beery's "The Champ" has any American picture striven so hard for a feeling of place. The choice of Phil Stong's novel was of course an excellent one for the purpose. Certainly nothing offers a better opportunity for the localization of distinctive American types, situations, and *mores* [customs] than a Middle Western state fair. There is a stretch in which we follow a typical American family riding at night along the corn fields, which has something of the beauty we admire in Russian films.

DIALOGUE AND SOUND

Another review by Welford Beaton of the *Hollywood Spectator* deals rather bitingly with the use of dialogue and sound:

> Jimmy Durante screams his way through the endless reels of "What—No Beer?," a comedyless comedy made by Metro, directed by Edward Sedgwick, featuring Buster Keaton and Durante, and being graced by the presence in the cast of Phyllis Barry, an attractive Australian girl who has both good looks and ability. She is this depressing comedy's one redeeming feature.
>
> The fact that Robert Hopkin's original story is a silly one and that Carey Wilson's screen play made from it has in itself no merit, does not excuse the lack of merit in the production. For the rollicking sort of comedy it was supposed to be, the story is of little account. What is needed is a sense of humor in its treatment. The picture lacks humor.
>
> To start with, I can not understand how Metro executives can expect an audience to be entertained by Durante's screaming all the way through a feature-length comedy. His voice finally becomes so irritating that I almost was prompted to do some screaming on my own hook. In addition to that irritation, there is a continuous barrage of other discordant noises until the thing becomes a cinematic nightmare that will not induce an audience to laugh loud enough at any point to drown the din that comes from the screen.

A COMPLETE REVIEW OF "OLIVER TWIST"

I should like to point out that a reviewer may not necessarily deal with all of these topics when he writes his review. You may expect, however, that if any phases of the motion picture are outstandingly strong or weak, he will comment upon them.

You can well afford to spend a good deal of time selecting reviews of different pictures and of the same picture, in order to discover just what it is that reviewers include in their discussions. For example, you might select five different reviews of the same picture and have members of your class rate them independently, let us say, into five groups. Each person should keep his rating secret and at the end you may find it very interesting to see how well you agree.

I include here a review of "Oliver Twist" by Welford Beaton to give you a sample of a fine type of review.

One of the finest collections of first editions in Hollywood is that owned by I. E. Chadwick, who has been producing motion pictures now and then since a long time ago. He has a number of Dickens first editions—those containing the Cruikshank drawings which were approved by Dickens himself as representing authentically the spirit of the tales they illustrated. Dickens approved not only the general composition and architecture, but also the costumes on the characters as the artist had visualized them. Thus the Cruikshank drawings became accepted as an authentic part of the Dickens books.

One day Chadwick took his *Oliver Twist* in hand. Were there enough lovers of Dickens in the world to make it profitable to put the real Dickens on the screen? He thought there were. Anyway, he took a chance. More, perhaps, than the characters of any other writer, those of Dickens lent themselves to picturesque effectiveness on the screen, his scenes are graphic, and *Oliver Twist* is a richly human story.

The book was given to Elizabeth Meehan and the Cruikshank drawings to Ernest Hickson. William J. Cowen was engaged as director.

Miss Meehan sketched accurately the seven hundred pages of the book into a narrative of screen length, Hickson recreated the Cruikshank drawings in beaverboard, lumber, and paving stones; the Cruikshank costumes were reproduced down to the smallest details, and Cowen brought the whole thing to the screen, giving us the truest Dickens that ever has been presented outside his books.

Oliver Twist in its motion picture form is an artistic achievement of which its producer has a right to be proud. There is very little dialogue in it and what there is is copied verbatim from the book. Cowen's direction preserves admirably the spirit of Dickens. He does what few of our directors seem able to do—he makes silence reasonable. In the scenes in which the characters do not talk, he presents them to us in a manner that makes talk unnecessary.

My only criticism of the picture is that it lacks a musical score. Its long, silent sequences would be much more effective if they were provided with a musical accompaniment.

The performances are in capable hands. Dickie Moore makes an appealing Oliver Twist. That sterling actor, Irving Pichel, gives a superbly artistic characterization of Fagin. William Boyd from the stage brings Bill Sikes to life in a vivid manner. Alec B. Francis as Mr. Brownlow and Doris Lloyd as Nancy give splendid performances. Roy Hunt's photography is of a high order.

The Composite Motion-Picture Critic

Some time ago the *Film Daily*, a magazine written for producers, exhibitors, and others in the motion-picture business, sent out a questionnaire to three hundred of the nation's foremost film critics. The tabulation of the results of this questionnaire gives you a picture of the activities and ideas of these critics. These results are as follows:

The composite, or average motion-picture critic:

Sees an average of 197 films a year.

Defends his right to express his personal viewpoint in reviews, instead of taking audiences into account.

Considers the director the most important element in motion-picture production; writers, second; players, third.

Sees no demand for silent pictures.

Does not consider current screen entertainment too sophisticated.

Believes present-day theater advertising is inclined to over-exaggerate and mislead.

Thinks the producers could make the most improvement in stories.

Is opposed to playing more than one full-length feature on a program.

Favors travelogues above all types of short subjects; cartoons, second; newsreels, third.

Is peeved most over "cycles," and almost equally as much over changes made in popular novels and plays adapted to the screen; and suggests "less sex" as his pet theory on films.

What Is the Value of the Review?

Can we depend *entirely* upon newspaper reviewers to give us good criticisms either of a particular motion picture or of the art of making motion pictures? Many motion-picture reviews are written in such haste that their authors are likely to give inaccurate and misleading notions of the picture. Such reviewers, even if able, suffer from another handicap. Newspapers and magazines attempt to make the widest possible appeal. Therefore, their motion-picture reviewers will try to interest the general reader whose reactions to a motion picture are usually either of two extremes: "I liked it" or "I did not like it." They say little or nothing about the motion picture as art, as the skillful interpretation of important experience.

Further, the motion-picture exhibitor advertises in the paper in which the reviews appear. If the critic is too honest about the poor quality of many motion pictures, the exhibitor may decide to give his advertising to a paper which has a less critical movie reviewer. Therefore we realize that reviews may sometimes be more favorable than they should be so that the advertisers will not be offended.

Shall we dismiss the newspaper reviews, then, as a source of information about films? Not at all. A few daily newspapers have men on their staffs who write for the thoughtful reader. This means, however, that their reviews may be technical and not understood by everyone, but what of that? Those parts of the newspaper which deal with music, painting, and finance are not well understood by every reader. They are published, however, because there are persons who purchase papers just to read these departments. If the editors of the papers believed that a better type of motion-picture review was demanded by their readers, they would furnish it.

What is a good motion-picture review? A good motion-picture review must meet certain standards of good writing. The writer ought to have something important to say about the interpretation of the motion picture. Of course, all of the different areas of motion-picture criticism cannot be covered in one review, but significant facts which relate to the picture being reviewed should be discussed. If reviewers fail to do this, either they are writing less well than they know how, or they are not capable.

PROBLEMS AND ACTIVITIES

1. Do you read reviews of pictures which you do not attend? Why?
2. Have your standards for a good picture changed as you grew older? Explain.
3. Should all motion pictures be fit for children to see? Explain.
4. Can there be just one set of standards to be applied to a motion picture which would definitely label it as good, bad, or indifferent? Would one be desirable?
5. Should all the books in a good library be suitable for children to read? Why?
6. Do you discuss the movie with other members of your family before or after you have seen it? How?
7. Develop a bulletin board of motion-picture reviews.
8. Score pictures on a one- to four-star basis and see how well

members of your class or a group of your friends agree on what they call a good picture.

9. Write reviews of current motion pictures and post them on the bulletin board.

10. Arrange for your newspaper to print motion-picture reviews in every issue. If these are too late to be useful, take extracts from good motion-picture reviews presented by newspapers and magazines.

11. Participate in school history projects relating to the historical accuracy of so-called historical motion pictures.

CHAPTER VI

THE STORY

WHERE DOES THE STORY COME FROM?

HAVE you ever wondered where the motion-picture producers get the stories which they film? You recognize some of them, of course, as adaptations from well-known books and plays, but perhaps you never thought much about the source of the others. Now, the quality of a story bears some relation to the source from which it was taken. Therefore, you will probably be interested in becoming familiar with these sources, and you may discover that your motion-picture enjoyment and appreciation will be increased by learning to evaluate pictures according to type.

There are two common sources: first, stories or plays not written originally for the screen; and second, "screen plays" or stories written for the motion pictures. In the first group are included all pictures made from books, novels, short stories, dramas old and new, musical comedies, light operas, and the like. Those in the second group need no explanation; they are simply original stories written directly for the screen.

INDIRECT SOURCES OF STORIES

The motion pictures based on well-known stories are generally easily recognized since the material used has already had some publicity. Of course, books and plays less well known are sometimes purchased and adapted or "doctored up" in some way. At any rate, here are a few examples of motion pictures made from stories or plays not written

74

originally for the screen, although some of them were given
new names: "Tom Sawyer," "Broken Lullaby" (originally
"The Man I Killed"), "Huck Finn," "Strangers in Love"
(originally "The Shorn Lamb"), "Tarzan," "Grand Hotel,"
"An American Tragedy," "Arrowsmith," "The Sin of
Madelon Claudet" (titled "Lullaby" when first released,
but later changed), "Cimarron," and "The Wet Parade."
All of these film stories were originally published in book
form, and one or two, such as *An American Tragedy,* were
also dramatized for the legitimate stage.

High-school students are often interested in seeing a
favorite book or play made into a movie. Here are some of
the books that high-school students in Cincinnati wanted to
see made into motion pictures:

All Quiet on the West- ern Front	Lady of the Lake
	Little Women
An Old Fashioned Girl	Lorna Doone
Anne of Green Gables	Prince and the Pauper
Ben-Hur	Richard Carvel
Call of the Wild	Seventeen
Count of Monte Cristo	Tale of Two Cities
Crisis, The	Tarzan of the Apes
David Copperfield	Tom Sawyer
Gentleman from Indiana	Trail of the Lonesome Pine
Girl of the Limberlost	Treasure Island
Ivanhoe	Twenty Thousand Leagues
Kidnapped	under the Sea

As you read through this list you will see that several
of the books have already been made into motion pictures.
"All Quiet on the Western Front," for example, was tremendously successful, and it is estimated that this picture
has been seen by 35,000,000 Americans and possibly 30,000,-
000 Europeans. "Little Women," and "Treasure Island,"
are now under production, and may be released by the time

that you read this paragraph. "Tom Sawyer" was produced in 1931 and was a highly successful picture.   A few other stories on this list have also been filmed.

There is another subdivision of the first group: dramas which have been made into motion pictures.   With the development of "talkies," there was a great rush to purchase stage plays, although many plays had previously been filmed. Today, every playwright realizes that, if his play should have a successful run in New York, some motion-picture producer may wish to purchase it.   Some of the plays which have been made into motion pictures during 1931, 1932, and 1933 are: "Private Lives," "Tomorrow and Tomorrow," "Five Star Final," "The Front Page," "The Spider," "Street Scene," "The Guardsman," "The Taming of the Shrew," "Rebound," "Strictly Dishonorable," "Strange Interlude," "Dinner at Eight," and "One Sunday Afternoon."

When motion pictures with sound were first being developed, there was also a great demand for musical comedies, light operas, and operettas, many of which were filmed much as they originally were presented, but this was not a wholly successful undertaking. Examples of these musical productions are "Rio Rita," "Hit the Deck," "New Moon," "Topsy and Eva," "The Cocoanuts," "The Vagabond King," and "The Student Prince." A photographed musical comedy is not necessarily a successful motion picture. There is little doubt, however, that music is going to be one of the chief additions to good motion pictures. Perhaps musical comedies eventually will be made successfully into good motion pictures, but the future of this effort is at present not easily predicted.   The success of "42nd Street" is probably due to the fact that it was written for the camera and was not merely a photograph of a musical comedy as seen on the typical stage. Many of the shots, for example,

Paramount

PETER PAN

This story by J. M. Barrie lent itself readily to motion-picture treatment.

were taken from an angle which would be denied the spectator of a musical comedy; some of them were above the
dancing, and at other times the stage used was much wider
than the ordinary stage. The songs were broken up by bits
of action. In other words, the picture moved.

STORIES WRITTEN DIRECTLY FOR THE SCREEN

In the second class of films—stories written directly for
the screen—are "Scarface," "The Secret Six," "Symphony
of Six Million," "City Lights," "Hell's Angels," "The
Champ," "Sky Devils," "Horse Feathers," and "Feet
First." Often these stories are written for a certain motion-
picture star. Others are written and directed by the star
himself; for example, "City Lights" was written and directed
by the star, Charlie Chaplin, and "Feet First" was similarly
directed by Harold Lloyd. Incidentally, films of this type
sometimes represent a growth; that is, the author, the director, and the star will start out with the skeleton of a plot and
will add many situations and much of the dialogue in the
course of the filming. Naturally, the only sort of film that
lends itself well to this sort of construction is a comedy such
as those mentioned. Most "screen stories," however, are
quite definitely worked out before the actual filming is
commenced.

STUDIO	NUMBER OF WOMEN WRITERS	NUMBER OF MEN WRITERS	TOTAL
M-G-M...................	16	54	70
Paramount................	3	36	39
Columbia.................	5	27	32
Universal.................	3	26	29
Radio....................	3	21	24
Warners..................	2	16	18
Fox.....................	4	12	16
Total................	36	192	228

There are a large number of writers attached to the Hollywood studios. The table on page 79 taken from the magazine *Variety* presents the number of writers under contract to major studios on June 25, 1932.

Advantages and Disadvantages of Different Sources

One of the reasons motion-picture producers are willing to pay large sums of money for successful plays, when original stories can be purchased at lower cost, is explained by Bertram Block, editor of the eastern dramatic department of Metro-Goldwyn-Mayer, in an article which appeared in the *New York Times:*

> In the case of an enormous stage success, there is naturally the matter of prestige, the fact that the title of a long run play is widely known throughout the country as the result of the publicity it has received. Then, too, one may assume that if a story has interested a considerable number of people in one acted form it will interest them in another. And there is also the consideration that the story has been completely worked out, and that it has already tested audience reactions. These are what may be called the obvious advantages.
>
> But there are subtler advantages that a play which has been given Broadway production possesses over an original story. One of these is that a dramatist puts in more work on a play than a writer does on a story constructed especially for the screen. The play will run 120 pages and may represent a year's effort. It is the sincere attempt of a playwright in a medium of expression which he considers important and with which his reputation is connected. He has put everything into those 120 pages, every bit of emotion, thought, dialogue, and business, down to the last detail. He has written it as something he wanted to say.
>
> On the other hand, an original story for the screen covers thirty pages; it is largely a synopsis. Most authors write for the screen with their left hand. They are interested in the money rather than sincerely moved to tell a story or express an idea.[1]

[1] Bamberger, Theron, "Will the Films Buy It?" *New York Times*, April 3, 1932.

This is not complimentary to the screen writer, is it? But did you ever hear of an author winning great fame by writing stories for the screen? How many screen writers do you know? Have you heard of Frances Marion, of Hans Kraly, of Adela Rogers St. John, of Ernest Pascal, of Gregory La Cava, of Willard Mack, of George Marion, Jr., of Agnes Brand Leahy? Frances Marion, who wrote the scenarios for "The Champ," "Secret Six," and "Emma," is perhaps the best known. Yet you are probably acquainted with the names of Philip Barry, Elmer Rice, Eugene O'Neill, Noel Coward, and others who have written well-known stage plays that were later made into motion pictures.

But why are the screen writers not so well known as the authors of stage successes? Is it true that screen writers are "interested in the money rather than sincerely moved to tell a story or express an idea?" Miss Helen Penland, who has been associated for a number of years with one of the major producing companies, replied to these criticisms as follows:

> Can you expect a scenario writer to be a creative genius when he spends all his time either doing adaptations of books and plays or carrying out the producer's ideas? If, once in a great while, a staff writer does submit his pet creation, it is either immediately disregarded or it is looked upon as a doubtful undertaking because it has not yet been produced on the stage or published in book form.
>
> The producers are taking no chances on unproven material—except in rare instances—and then they so flood the story with their own ideas until it in no way resembles the original story. A contract means big money in Hollywood, and the writer does what he is told to do, or gets out.
>
> Do not blame the writers, but the "system" which, considering the money risk, you cannot blame too much either. The solution to better motion pictures is the public, of course, and

second, there should be more production in New York studios, where talent can be obtained without long-time, expensive contracts, and where original ideas would not be at such a premium. The stage and screen could then work out their ideas together, to their mutual advantage.

Welford Beaton says almost the same thing:

> As far as I have learned from working with several of them, writers are not too prone to lean heavily on past successes, but I find that it is difficult to get an idea past a producer or a supervisor if it has not already been proved successful in some picture that has been produced.[1]

"But," we may ask, "isn't it possible for a screen writer to spend as much time in writing a screen play as a playwright does in composing a drama? Why should not the screen writer consider his medium of expression just as important as the playwright does his? Could not one make a reputation by writing screen stories as well as by writing plays? Could not a screen writer set down his story as 'something he wanted to say,' and include in it 'every bit of emotion, thought, dialogue, and business, down to the last detail'?" Perhaps the day may come when good screenwriting will win just as much fame as good play-writing; when the names of able screen writers will be as well known as those of Barry, O'Neill, Coward, and other playwrights.

Good Writers Must Know What the Camera Can Do

There is a feeling among those who are familiar with scenarios that good writing for the screen can come only from those who are thoroughly familiar with the possibilities and the limitations of motion pictures. They believe that a writer who is a novelist or dramatist can never success-

---

[1] *Hollywood Spectator*, April 20, 1929, p. 3.

fully write for the screen because he has trained himself to write in another medium. It is true, of course, that we can expect to have many adaptations; however, there does seem to be a need for able screen writers. One wonders, therefore, if this need will ever adequately be fulfilled. While it may be true that many able scripts are done by screen writers, nevertheless the prestige of the screen writer is often so slight that it is doubtful if persons will be willing to train themselves adequately for this instead of aspiring to success in writing novels or dramas.

Iris Barry says:

> I have come lately, however, to feel that established writers of fiction and plays are too much wedded to their own medium to be successful in adapting themselves to writing for the films. The best scenarios are written by men who know how films are made; who know what can be done effectively and what can not. And it certainly looks as if this experience of practical cinematography were almost essential to the making of a live photoplay. After all, Shakespeare and Molière were men of the theater and it did them no harm. So in the film studios will arise men of peculiar talent for this new form, having at their fingers' ends an instinctive knowledge of its possibilities and innate beauties.[1]

Much of the responsibility for this change, however, will lie in the hands of the motion-picture reviewers. Have you ever read a review of a good stage play in which there was no mention made of the author? And yet it is seldom that the author's name is included in a motion-picture review. To that extent, every film review is only a partial review. Moreover, every motion picture has in a sense two authors— the screen writer and the director—and each should be mentioned.

[1] Barry, Iris, *Let's Go to the Movies*, pp. 163–164.

Problems Faced in Adapting Books and Plays

There are many difficulties encountered in adapting books and plays to the screen. In the first place, the mediums of the stage and the screen are different. The meaning of the play upon the stage depends primarily upon words; the movie, upon pictures. Each of them has certain, and different, limitations. A stage play must be so handled that what is said or done by the actors can be understood by persons seated in the balcony and in the gallery quite a distance from the stage. Sometimes some of the best lines may not be heard.

But at the movies every action is visible to every spectator, since it takes place on what might be thought of as a movable stage, one which comes closer or moves farther away from the spectator as the situation demands. Another difference is that the success of a stage play must depend largely on its dialogue, while it is possible to produce a good motion picture with little or no dialogue. Also, the action in a stage play is usually confined to a few scenes, while there is practically no limitation, except perhaps that of cost, to the sets used in a motion picture. Therefore, because of these differences, the adaptation of plays to movies is not always successful.

Are adaptations of books usually well made? Sometimes they are, sometimes they are not. Often there is a failure to keep the spirit of the original. High-school students are sometimes very skillful at discovering this. Here are some of their comments about the motion picture "David Copperfield," made from the book of that name. "David Copperfield" was a silent picture, and up to the time of the writing of this book (1933) had not been refilmed in sound. These comments are furnished by Miss Marian Dogherty in her book, *Literature in the Schools*. One high-school student said:

I missed the part where Dora takes account of her housekeeping in the kind of food she gives David. Uriah Heep should have been more untidy. He should have the appearance of one who makes people feel creepy.

Another comment was made about Uriah Heep, and this person says:

I liked the picture, but it seemed to me that Uriah Heep was not so humble as he was in the book.

Another student said:

There's one thing I didn't like very much and that was when David's dear wife Dora dies, and David was shown making love right off to Agnes. Anybody who didn't read the book wouldn't have known that David waited three years before he married Agnes. David was really blind when he married Dora, for Agnes's love was greater. However, the picture as a whole was worth-while, and I wouldn't have missed it for anything.

And here's the last one I'll quote:

One thing that I did not like was the quick changing of years in the picture, without having incidents happen to lead up to them.[1]

These comments have been introduced for two reasons. In the first place, they show that high-school students are thinking about what they see on the screen. In the second place, they show the difficulty of putting the written word into pictures. Adapting a book or play to the screen is a doubly hard task. One must know how to make the necessary changes, so that the spirit and flavor of the original book or play are not lost.

Remember, then, that there may logically be some changes

[1] Dogherty, Marian Agnes, *Literature in the Schools*, pp. 59–62.

from the original story. But every change ought to justify itself, and no changes should be made just because there is a notion among some producers that the motion picture ought always be changed somewhat from the book. It is just as wrong, of course, to believe that no changes should ever be made. Books cannot be made directly into pictures since some of the events in a book cannot be satisfactorily pictured.

What Is a Good Story?

The quality and nature of a story will be influenced by its source. The story must, however, be rated on points other than this. What are some other necessary qualities of a good motion-picture story?

A good motion-picture story must really do what it sets out to do. If the producers of a picture have led you to believe through their advertising that their films say something important about crime, politics, war, love, or religion, then the pictures must say something that is really important. They ought to give you an honest interpretation of these important problems which will be significant for your life, furnish you a sympathetic insight into the lives of persons who have differing standards of conduct, and truthfully show you the consequences of having those standards.

Of course, many motion pictures have another purpose. They do not pretend to say anything important. On the contrary, they aim to say something funny, to put you in a good humor, to make you laugh. A worthy aim, is it not? Here the first standard for judging the effectiveness of the story is whether it was really funny. Further, one must next inquire whether the humor thus gained was in good taste. Was it vulgar? Was it secured at the expense of some particular race or group of people?

Drunkenness, for example, is frequently used in the motion pictures in order to create humor. Many people, including the writer, sometimes think it is funny. You will perhaps agree with the criticism which a reviewer made of such scenes in one motion picture:

> In order to let you know that I am not assuming a holier-than-thou attitude, I confess that I found the drunken sequence extremely amusing, but that does not alter the fact that it is not the wholesome, clean entertainment that pictures heretofore have carried into the homes of the world.[1]

Motion pictures commonly get humorous effects by showing us the dumb Swede; the affected Englishman with his monocle, spats, and frock coat; the mincing, dandified, effeminate Frenchman. Many of us have learned to laugh at these stereotypes. But persons belonging to these nationalities do not usually find these characters funny, nor should we enjoy the humor of the foreign version of an American—the go-getting businessman, crude in his manners, who uses a Yankee twang and an unbelievable number of slang expressions.

I do not mean to suggest that satire has no place in the movies or that motion pictures should be forever smugly pointing out a moral. They do, however, show how people live; and that way of living is usually presented to the persons who view that picture as approved or disapproved. The movies teach lessons, therefore, whether the producers intend it or not.

For example, you could not help feeling, after seeing "All Quiet on the Western Front" and "Broken Lullaby," that war is a disastrous and wholly unnecessary part of our civilization. "Emma" pictured for us the love and devotion of a nurse and stepmother to the children under her care.

---

[1] *Hollywood Spectator*, May 4, 1929, p. 9.

I think many children and youth would see their mothers in a new light after viewing this picture, for there was a great deal in it for them to think about. "Wet Parade" made many people think seriously about their relationship to the problem of prohibition, and it gave them some ideas that they could use in building a way of life.

The Plot and Its Development

The plot of a story, and this refers to the situations which are included in it, should be plausible and reasonable, unless it is slapstick comedy, burlesque, farce, or fantasy. There are many pictures the plots of which are so improbable that a thinking person's reaction to them cannot help but be unfavorable. Not all people, of course, will agree as to the intelligence or unintelligence of the actions of certain characters on the screen.

An illustration of a poorly worked-out plot was "The Wild Party," in which the heroine made a sacrifice for her roommate in a situation that could have been simply and easily explained to the school authorities. Another implausible plot is found in the picture "Father and Son." The whole story hinges on the fact that the father bought a recording phonograph for his son, and this phonograph was turned on at the moment when his stepmother was killed. The young son thought his father killed the mother, and the father thought that the son killed the mother. As the story unfolds on the screen, one feels that it could not have happened. Still another example of a plot based on an extremely improbable situation is the picture "Scotland Yard." An ugly, scarred criminal steals the picture of a beautiful girl and her husband. He enlists in the army, his face is badly shattered by shrapnel, and the only clue to his former appearance is a picture found on his person,

FAREWELL TO ARMS   *Paramount*
    Some of the leading characters discussing the script.

believed by others to be of himself. The plastic surgeon remakes his face to the pattern of the pictured man, and the criminal returns to London, where he passes himself off as the other man, an English banker.

These examples are from pictures that you probably have not seen, but they resemble weaknesses which you may discover in the pictures you are seeing. The point to remember is that sensible and intelligent plot situations are as good for plot construction as unintelligent ones, and to many people plausible situations are far more interesting. Unreasonable plots, such as have been discussed, weaken the story for the intelligent movie-goer.

PLOT VERSUS TREATMENT

If you continue to read a good deal about dramatic criticism, you will find much discussion about the importance of plot and its relationship to the treatment of the story. You will find that some writers depend a good deal upon intricate and complicated plots, while others use simple ones and depend for their effects upon the skillful treatment of simple happenings.

Here, for example, is what Frances Marion, the well-known screen writer, says about the plot of the screen story:

> Plot today does not mean so much as characterization and the little incidental touches that embellish a picture. The letter episode in "The Big House," where Wallace Beery pretends to his fellow-convicts that the news of his mother's death is a love letter from a girl, is an example. Here the audience sympathizes with the tragedy in the heart of the great hulking brute who forces a grin lest his fellow-men see the anguish in his heart.[1]

[1] Lewin, William, "Standards of Photoplay Appreciation," *The English Journal,* December, 1932, pp. 799–810.

Is it possible that motion pictures are going into a decline because of a lack of new and different plots? Some persons have said that this was the cause of the decline in interest in silent pictures just before sound and speech were added to them. They pointed out that the themes of wide appeal had been exhausted.

Mr. I. A. Richards, one of the greatest modern literary critics, says in his book, *Principles of Literary Criticism*, that,

> Perhaps the chief reason for the decline of the drama in the seventeenth century (social factors apart) was the exhaustion of the best themes which could be used in order to appeal at all levels. Drama, to secure audiences large enough to be encouraging, must make a wide-spread appeal; but the limitations which this condition imposes upon action are very strict.[1]

If it is true that an art medium can exhaust its themes of wide appeal, then the motion picture must begin to depend more upon treatment of the story than upon the plot.

How Achieve Suspense?

The development of suspense is an important element in motion-picture construction, and, if carefully worked out, will result in such an unfolding of the plot that the spectator will not be able to forecast exactly what is going to happen. If he is sure of all the incidents which will occur in the picture, and just how the story will turn out, he soon becomes bored by it. The intelligent movie-goer naturally dislikes seeing the same old plot and the same old situations again and again. A well-constructed play will hold his attention from beginning to end. It will not be difficult to follow, and yet it will not be so simple as to be dull.

When King Vidor wished to show that Zeke, the leading

---

[1] Richards, I. A., *Principles of Literary Criticism*, p. 214.

character in "Hallelujah," had been sent to prison for murder, he used only two scenes: a group of Negro convicts working on a rock pile, and a close-up of Zeke. One saw no arrest, no trial, no sentence. A typical movie director would have treated the audience to a scene showing the arrest of Zeke, with close-ups of Zeke in his cell and a smashing climax at his conviction. But King Vidor is an able director. He knew that these scenes were unnecessary for the advancement of the plot, and would only have slowed the picture down; since they would have added nothing to it, he wisely left them out.

The death of the young married couple in "Cavalcade" was told convincingly by merely one scene. They are on the deck of the *Titanic*, a steamer which was rammed by an iceberg in 1912. The tragedy is foretold when the young couple step aside, revealing a life preserver with the name, *Titanic*, printed on it.

One valuable method which directors use to intensify interest in a picture is to set the stage for some dramatic event and then to let time elapse before it happens. In other words, the spectator of the picture knows that something is going to happen and is disturbed about it mentally, a condition which the director is trying to bring about. Here are some examples. In "Arrowsmith" we see that some dangerous disease germs have been accidentally dropped on a cigarette. We know that some one is going to smoke that cigarette, and be subjected to great danger. We are, therefore, excited by the possibility—the effect the director is trying to achieve. Another method of handling this same situation is to put a character into a precarious position and then leave him while the story moves on to a different location. This was done in "Cimarron," where the Negro boy was shot. After he has been shot, the action goes on in another setting for a brief period; all the time, of course, the spectator is wondering what has happened to the boy. D. W. Griffith made excellent use of this device in his pictures, carrying two or three stories on simultaneously, and picking up now one, then another.

Should Comedy Relief Be Used?

The forward movement of a motion picture is sometimes slowed down by the mistaken notion on the part of the director that every serious play should have some comedy scenes.   But the effectiveness of such plays is sometimes lost by bringing in comedy which is wholly artificial. Indeed, humor is all too often secured by dragging in situations merely to get effects in no way connected with the story. The less obvious the attempt to bring in humor, the more effective it is.   It is true that a skillful dramatist may use humor to relieve the audience's feelings in a highly tense scene; but he must not use the humor before the tension is created, nor must the humor destroy the effect of that scene.

An outstanding example of badly used comedy relief was seen in "Fighting Caravans," in which Gary Cooper and Lili Damita played. The name of the picture and the advertising led one to believe that one would see on the screen a picturization of the problems faced in transporting goods overland to California in the early days.   We expected to see an epic of the West.   Here, indeed, was an excellent opportunity for skillful camera work and masterful portrayals. Instead, most of the footage was taken up with the unentertaining and drunken antics of Ernest Torrence and Tully Marshall.   This does not mean that there is no place for comedy in serious stories.   There is, indeed, a definite place when it fits naturally.   If it does not, it is best left out.

WHAT MOTION-PICTURE CRITICS SAY ABOUT THE STORIES

When the motion-picture critics of the country were asked the question, "In what respect could producers make the most improvement in pictures?" the following information was obtained:

> Stories are most in need of improvement, in the overwhelming opinion of the nation's critics. Fully 98 per cent of the several hundred film scribes participating in this questionnaire voluntarily mention story material, and a majority of them are quite hot about the matter.
>
> As a suggestion for putting the needed improvement into effect, more than a hundred critics urged the writing of more original stories conceived directly with a view to the requirements and possibilities of the screen.
>
> Too much use of dialogue instead of action is one of the chief criticisms of present stories. Illogical situations, fantastic plots and forced endings also brought numerous complaints, and writers are advised to stop trying to shock audiences and devote more effort to sincere human problems and natural emotions that all can understand. More wholesome stories about normal people are advocated.[1]

SUMMARY OF STANDARDS

Here are the standards which the writer sets up in this chapter for the story. If you do not agree with this set of standards, revise them to fit your own standards for a photoplay.

1. A good motion-picture story must really do what it sets out to do.
2. The story should be so built that there is a consistent rise in interest from the beginning of the picture until the climax.
3. A well-constructed motion picture should not be hard to follow or understand.

[1] *1932 Film Daily Directors' Annual and Production Guide*, p. 20.

4. Any problem which is presented in a serious motion picture should be presented accurately.
5. Such a picture might end happily or unhappily, as long as the ending is logical.
6. Humor in motion pictures should not be consistently built up at the expense of certain races or nationalities.
7. Further, the humor should fit naturally into the situation and should not be used merely as relief.
8. One of the most important things the motion picture can do is to show you truthfully the consequences that come from making certain choices in life.

QUESTIONS FOR REVIEW

Here are some questions that members of the class may wish to ask themselves after they have seen a photoplay. Perhaps your group can find other questions which they wish to add, or they may wish to change this list.

1. Was the title appropriate? If not, what do you think would have been a satisfactory one?
2. What was the writer's name? Have you seen other pictures written by the same author? How did this picture compare with them?
3. Was the story always believable? Why or why not?
4. If the story was adapted from a play or a novel, were there any changes which you thought were good or poor? If so, where?
5. Were the characters effectively introduced? How was it done?
6. Were the characterizations believable? Why?
7. At what points was the story especially realistic? Too artificial?
8. Did the author or director show unusual understanding of how people would act under different circumstances? Where?
9. Was the plot too simple? Too complicated? Satisfactory? Give reasons for your opinion.
10. Was interest maintained right up to the climax? If not, how

might the story have been changed in order to secure such interest?

11. If this story dealt with romantic love, did it do so in a new way, or did it follow the patterns of other pictures?

12. Was the ending logical? If not, might there have been a better ending? Suggest one.

13. Was the humor effectively introduced? Was it in good taste?

CHAPTER VII

ACTING

COMMENTS about the acting of motion-picture characters are common, since most persons prefer certain actors and actresses whose work they feel is usually of superior merit. One person's acting is liked because it is so real and human; another's is disliked because it is shallow—lacking in understanding. The suavity and smoothness of a particular actor may appeal to some; to others it seems artificial. We realize, therefore, that tastes in acting differ, and frequently that standards for judging the acting are also different. We come then to the question, "By what standards should we judge the acting which we see on the screen?"

Standards for acting are hard to set up, for they vary greatly from country to country. It is difficult, for example, for most Americans to appreciate the acting of Mei Lan-fang, the famous Chinese actor who recently toured this country, because in his acting certain gestures or movements have special meanings. Chinese drama is a kind of shorthand which you must know in order to understand what is happening. It is not natural, or what we call "realistic." Instead, it is symbolic. Which is the better standard? Today most of us prefer the naturalistic method, but that does not necessarily prove that it is better.

STANDARDS FOR GOOD ACTING

We can get good acting in a motion picture if we have the following conditions:

1. Proper casting
2. Satisfactory make-up
3. Intelligent understanding of the rôle
4. Skillful picturing of the necessary emotions
5. Naturalness in acting
6. Skillful use of dialogue
7. Proper timing
8. Sufficient dramatic build-up

1. Proper casting:

If a good actor or actress is cast in the wrong rôle, there is little he or she can do to make the character believable. Many good actors and actresses have failed to make a success in motion pictures because of the unsuitable rôles in which they were cast.

What are some standards for casting? First, we can expect that the actor's appearance should be reasonably in keeping with his rôle. In other words, Wallace Beery should not be cast as a dancing master, nor William Powell as a prize fighter, while Frederic March might not make a believable gangster.

Care must also be taken when casting a foreign actor or actress. We are greatly disturbed when a person who is supposed to speak pure English has a foreign accent. But Greta Garbo is very satisfactorily cast as the daughter of a Norwegian farmer in Minnesota, since under these circumstances her Swedish accent fits the part. She could also be cast as a Russian dancer, as in "Grand Hotel." She seemed well cast as the spy in "Mata Hari," but in that same picture Ramon Novarro's accent was disturbing, for it made the picture seem less real. The minute the spectator starts questioning the plausibility, that is, the believableness of the character, much of what follows in the play is lost. The actors and actresses must cast a spell, the magic spell of illusion. Unless they are sufficiently well fitted to their rôles to do this, the spectators will not fall into the spirit of the play.

Here are some other examples of miscasting. Anyone who saw Frederic March in "True to the Navy" with Clara Bow and in "Laughter" with Nancy Carroll will probably agree that he was better suited to the part of the talented musician in "Laughter" than he was to that of the sailor in "True to the Navy." And Clark Gable was not a convincing old man in "Strange Interlude." Your class may be interested in giving other examples of recent pictures where some of the leading characters seemed to be miscast.

Why do we have miscasting of characters? There are three reasons. First, the person selecting them may not understand the part; second, the producer may put a favorite actor into a rôle with the hope of bolstering up a weak play with a strong star; and third, players are under contract, and the producer loses money if they are left idle. Here's what Lee Tracy says about this matter in the *New York Times* for May 27, 1933: "Let me tell you something. I did eleven pictures in thirteen months before 'Dinner at Eight.' I was getting careless in my work. I was tired. I didn't care."

In casting, of course, one realizes that some actors have great versatility and range in their character impersonations. Among these are: Emil Jannings, Jean Hersholt, Helen Hayes, Irene Dunne, George Stone, Wallace Beery, Ruth Chatterton, and the late Lon Chaney. This list is by no means complete, and you may have your own favorites. Many actors do not have this ability and can give only a limited range of characterizations. Some one has pointed out that actors who have had a good deal of training in stock companies, that is, theatrical companies which produce a good many different plays, have much more versatility in acting than those who have played only one type of part.

Why do the character actors—Lewis Stone, Wallace Beery, Tully Marshall, Jean Hersholt, Alec B. Francis, Hobart Bosworth, Henry B. Walthall—long retain their popularity? Is it not due to the fact that they do not play themselves, but really play a character? Therefore, since there is freshness and vitality in each new picture they present, since we are likely to find them different, we do not tire of them. Most actors and actresses, however, play themselves only, and after a while we tire of seeing the same characterization.

2. Satisfactory make-up:

One of the not uncommon mistakes made by directors is the poor make-up of the characters. There has been (in several pictures) very poor use of make-up. In "Tomorrow and Tomorrow," Ruth Chatterton in several scenes had too much shadow around the eyes. In "Westward Passage," Ann Harding's eyes were also too dark and poor effects were obtained. In "Letty Lynton," Joan Crawford was made up so poorly that she looked, not beautiful, but unattractive and ghostlike. In "The Conquerors," when Richard Dix plays the part of the old man the make-up was noticeably artificial. Clark Gable's make-up as an old man in "Strange Interlude" was not convincing.

3. Intelligent understanding of the rôle:

Good acting must give evidence of an understanding of the part. An actor cannot truly impersonate a character unless he has carefully studied the play in which he is to appear. Jane Cowl, for example, studied and practiced the rôle of Juliet for several years before she was willing to try it on the stage. The motion-picture actress who plays this rôle, however, may study it only a few weeks. In the first case, the actress will have a complete understanding of the kind of person that Juliet is supposed to be. In the second, that understanding will be quite vague. Of course, under present studio conditions, when assignments are given only a few weeks in advance, it is sometimes impossible to study a character adequately.

The ablest directors, however, do try to enable their players to carry out such procedure. Ernst Lubitsch (see his photograph on page 183) receives this favorable comment:

> With his actors—whom he has usually selected long before he casts them—he expostulates one by one, a day for each, until they share to the last shade his reading of their parts. When the picture starts, he almost never changes anything.[1]

Under such training each player knows thoroughly the rôle which he is expected to play. Such an understanding among motion-picture actors, however, is probably more often the exception than the rule.

Good acting, then, is intelligent acting. Shakespeare emphasized the need for thinking when he had Hamlet instruct his players to "Suit the action to the word, the word to the action." Welford Beaton gives us some hints regarding standards for good acting when he speaks of Mae Marsh:

> She makes the mother a real person. There is not a flaw in her characterization. As the young mother in the opening sequence she is the animated housewife to the life, loving her children and her husband, and working from early to late. In the subsequent sequences she is one of the most adorable old women ever seen on the screen. It is in them that the part makes the greatest demands upon her. The underlying note of her performance is rare understanding. In one close-up showing her reaction to her son's sentence to prison, her eyes convey

[1] *Time*, February 1, 1932, p. 48.

to us the agony she feels. There are no tears, no facial distortions—just the eyes revealing the torture that must have been real to her when she was photographed.[1]

Another quotation from the *Hollywood Spectator* further defines good acting:

To give good performances, they (the actors and actresses) must lose themselves so thoroughly in the characterizations that they become the characters they play, and the measure of their success is the perfection they achieve in making the character natural.[2]

This same point of view is here presented in a little different way:

The late Fred Murnau said all there is to say in the way of advice to screen artists: "Don't act. Think." A director who can make his camera photograph the thoughts of the members of his cast must give us great pictures, provided he has actors who can think in terms of the parts they are playing. An actor who can think a scene will give a perfect performance in it. Automatically his physical actions will be in harmony with his thoughts.[3]

4. Skillful picturing of the necessary emotions:

Did you ever notice the bodily postures of a person who is experiencing strong emotion? Have you ever observed that a person who is sad does not have his shoulders thrown back, that his muscles are relaxed? That an excited or angry person, one who is ready to fight, has his muscles tense, his hands clenched? Watch people who are angry or frightened or disappointed to see what effect their emotions have upon them. From my window I have been watching a group of ten-year-old boys playing baseball. Although they are about a city block away, and I am unable to hear their words, I

[1] *Hollywood Spectator*, December, 1931, pp. 12–13.
[2] *Op. cit.*, p. 19.
[3] *Op. cit.*, November, 1931, p. 8.

can see that the boy at bat is angry with the pitcher. I am certain that he is angry, because of the position of his body, and the way he hits the ground with his bat; it is not the way a boy ordinarily hits the ground when he is waiting for the ball.

Certain emotions are accompanied by particular facial expressions and bodily postures. We might expect, therefore, that a good actor would spend a great deal of time in perfecting his understanding of bodily positions and attitudes during different emotions suitable to the personality of a particular character and would develop subtly different ways of showing them. Good actors probably do this, while poor actors depend upon the stock ways of expressing emotions. Keep this in mind when you go to the movies.

5. Naturalness in acting:

Naturalness plays a larger part in screen acting than it does on the stage. If the actors on the stage conversed in the same tone that they would ordinarily use, they would probably not be heard. Instead, they must exaggerate not only the pitch of their voices, but also their emotions and gestures, because some members of the audience may be as far as a hundred feet away. Motion pictures, however, require a wholly different kind of acting; since the audience is, in imagination at least, only as far away as the lens of the camera, any reaction which is portrayed can be picked up by the camera just as it really occurred. That reaction may be ever so subtle, merely the flicker of an eyelash, yet a close-up can record it. On the stage, however, this is impossible.

There are some who believe, because of the greater ease of capturing naturalness, that acting in the movies requires less technique and training than acting on the stage. In

Courtesy of the Metro-Goldwyn-Mayer Corp.

LIONEL BARRYMORE IN A VARIETY OF RÔLES

Note the hands, the skillful make-up, and the expressive eyes and mouth.
1. "Grand Hotel"; 2. "Looking Forward"; 3. "The Mysterious Island";
4. "Dinner at Eight"; 5. "Rasputin and the Empress"; 6. "Guilty Hands."

other words, that there are certain "naturals" as far as screen acting is concerned. Indeed, some Russian directors pick their cast from the street and rely upon their skill in teaching them how to interpret the necessary rôles. Marie Seton reports in the June, 1933, issue of *Close-up*,[1] that:

> When Pudovkin is preparing a picture he has five assistants who search for suitable types of people. Anywhere and everywhere they look for this human material which he will study for weeks before shooting, talking to them for hours and trying to understand their psychology. "You can't work with someone you don't know," he says. He will then shoot them in a hundred different poses for one small episode.

Now good acting is always natural acting, but does this mean acting natural? Perhaps this statement needs further explanation. When Helen Hayes acts natural, she is Helen Hayes and no one else. When she takes the part of some character in a motion picture, however, she must not act natural, but must resemble as much as possible the character whose rôle she is impersonating. The actor must be, not himself, but the character.

Acting, as we shall use it here, usually means that a person is trying to take a rôle other than himself. He is trying to make believe. In other words, he is trying to make you believe that he is the character he is portraying. That, then, is the chief standard for good acting—it must be good make-believe. It must make you believe that the actor is the character he is trying to portray.

The final impression that we should get of a character, then, is one of naturalness. The best actor is the one who seems to be acting the least. In *Tom Jones*, a book written by Fielding, Mr. Partridge is replying to the critics who

[1] This magazine may be obtained, at a cost of 15 shillings per year, by addressing *Close-up*, 26 Litchfield Street, Charing Cross Road. W.C.2, London, England.

have said that Hamlet was well played by David Garrick. Mr. Partridge snorts scornfully:

> He the best player! Why, I could act as well as he myself. I am sure, if I had seen a ghost, I should have looked in the same manner, and done just as he did. And then, to be sure, in that scene, as you called it, between him and his mother, where you told me he acted so fine, why, Lord help me, any man, that is, any good man, that had such a mother, would have done exactly the same. I know you are only joking with me; but indeed, madam, though I was never to a play in London, yet I have seen acting before in the country; and the king for my money; he speaks all his words distinctly, half as loud again as the other. Anybody may see he is an actor.[1]

Here we have a very good indication of what acting ought to be in spite of the fact that Mr. Partridge, who is speaking, has apparently a wrong notion about the matter.

But do we go to the theater to see Helen Hayes, or do we go to see her as she interprets a certain rôle? The editor of *Photoplay* thinks that we go just to see the actor or actress. Do you agree? He says:

> Other generations went to the theater to see Booth as *Othello;* Mansfield as *Cyrano* and Bernhardt as *Camille.*
>
> But we go to see Garbo as *Garbo.*
>
> Interpretations don't mean so much to us. Even George Arliss' characterizations do not impress like the man himself. And whether he plays a Hindu rajah, as in "The Green Goddess," or *Disraeli*, Arliss is pretty much himself—the same gestures, the same sly look of the eye when he delivers a telling line, the same facial expressions for similar emotional import.
>
> A great technician, it is true, but, withal, George Arliss. And George Arliss is what we want.[2]

[1] Fielding, Henry, *Tom Jones*, Vol. II, p. 413.
[2] Dougherty, Kathryn, "Close-Ups and Long-Shots," *Photoplay*, Vol. XLIII, No. 1 (December, 1932), p. 26.

6. Skillful use of dialogue:

The motion picture "Tom Sawyer" gives us an example of especially skillful use of dialogue. One of the delightful bits occurs when Tom, who has been unjustly punished for breaking a sugar bowl, meets his friend Joe, who has been forced to put on his Sunday clothes and carry a basket to a social. Both are in low spirits, and each delivers a monologue on his own troubles, paying no attention to what the other says:

"Makin' me fix up jus' so's I could bring this basket down to the social," Joe grumbles.

"Aw, they make me sick!" declares Tom.

Joe sighs. "If you had these shoes on your feet, I betcha you'd be sick."

"Old sugar bowl!" Tom snorts, paying no attention to Joe's comment.

They climb through a fence, Joe still growling, "Shoes, this time of year!"

"Wasn't no good, nohow," Tom mutters to himself.

"I didn't mind washin' my feet, but shoes—"

"Even if I had of busted it, it was all cracked and full of nicks."

"You'd think there was snow on the ground or somethin'—"

"They'd rather have you lie and be a tattle-tale—that's what they'd rather have you be."

This dialogue took place as the boys were walking along a road, and from time to time they would walk through or under a rail fence which was at the side of the road—the camera following their action all the while. As you read this aloud you will see that this is the kind of conversation that we would expect from boys the age of Joe and Tom.

Dialogue is nothing more than the usual speech of the characters in the story, and it becomes ineffective when it is unnatural or stilted. You should judge the dialogue of a play by its naturalness just as you would judge ordinary conversation. We should expect the Italian laboring man who has just come over to this country to speak broken English. If he speaks excellent English, we should be greatly astonished. If children appear in the picture, they ought to talk as children ordinarily talk, and yet there are errors in motion pictures on both these points.

Many motion pictures have another fault in their use of sound. There is too much useless talking. In silent pictures there was no talking at all, and as a result a great deal of skill was used by the director in developing meaning. When he found it impossible to convey meaning by means of what the characters did, he used a title. He tried hard, however, to avoid titles. At the present time it is so easy to have a character say something instead of do something that the directors sometimes blunder in this regard. If words alone can carry the story satisfactorily, then the script is better fitted for a radio drama than for a motion picture.

7. Proper timing:

Conrad Nagel, the well-known screen actor, has this to say about timing:

> The most important thing about any performance whether on the stage or on the screen, is sincerity. The next most important thing is an element entirely technical, the timing in an actor's performance. The great difference between the performance of the professional and the amateur artist is almost entirely one of timing. The amateur learns his lines and rambles through them, while the professional actor has learned to tell as much by his pauses, or by his timing, as with the actual words or gestures he may use. Timing is as important in the theatre as tempo is in music and punctuation in literature.[1]

[1] Lewin, William, "Standards of Photoplay Appreciation," *The English Journal*, December, 1932, pp. 799–810.

In the motion picture "Tom Sawyer," there were one or two examples of poor timing. One is where Becky is talking to Tom just after they have become engaged. Tom starts to mention something which happened when he was engaged to another girl, then pauses and waits until Becky breaks in and begins to cry. In real life, Tom would have kept on talking and wouldn't have stopped until Becky actually had begun to cry. But in the picture he anticipated her crying.

Another example of poor timing in that same play was the incident when Tom overhears the two women talking in front of Aunt Polly's house as he is leaving to return to Jackson's Island. You remember that he had left a note by Aunt Polly's bed, saying that he had run away to play pirate. He overhears the women talking about the plans to hold the funeral for the lost boys the next day, and at once he gets the idea of going back to get his letter, so that the three boys can attend their own funeral. Now, he got this idea too quickly. In real life we don't react that fast. Of course, I don't mean that motion pictures should always show an idea developing as slowly as it does in real life, but it should not give the spectator the feeling of too much speed. This particular error, however, should not be checked up against Jackie Coogan but against the director. He should have retaken this scene.

8. Sufficient dramatic build-up:

The best acting in the world will not put a scene over unless the dramatist and the cameraman have carefully prepared you for it. Why do certain notable scenes fail; even though the acting itself may be superb? They fail because we are uninterested in what is going to happen.

May I give an example of a scene in "Sweepings," in

which Lionel Barrymore appeared? Persons to whom I talked were not deeply touched by the death scene. Why? Not because the acting was poor; it was good. But we were unmoved because we didn't care much whether that person died or not, and the only way that we could learn to care was to know that other persons cared greatly. However, the dramatist had not convinced us that the death of the mother meant a great deal to the other persons in the story—the father and the four little children. In other words, the dramatist failed to tell what the death of the mother meant to the family. What did it mean? It meant that the father would be left to care for the four little children. It meant that the mother would never have the opportunity to see her four children grow up. It meant that the fine plans which she and her husband had drawn up for the store were ruined.

The incident of death in itself may have little effect upon our emotions unless it is accompanied by a richness of detail in reference to what such a death means. For example, when George Arliss in "The Working Man" asks Bette Davis the simple question as to whether or not she believes that she has followed the ideals of her dead mother, the latter begins to cry in a genuinely moving scene.

Illustrations of Good Acting

The only way to judge good acting is by its effects upon you. Do you feel sad when the director of the film is trying to convey a feeling of sadness, or do you laugh? For example, in one picture a young man was shown sobbing on his bed because he could not conquer his fear of going up in an airplane. His sobbing was not effective, as far as the audience was concerned, because as he sobbed, the audience laughed. Now there were two reasons why they laughed. First of all,

Paramount

Tom Sawyer

An old ne'er-do-well is on trial for murder. Note how expressive of despair is Tully Marshall's whole attitude.

the audience had not been well prepared for the scene by a
suitable sequence of previous scenes. They did not have
the right mental attitude for it. A second reason for their
failure to weep with the boy was the fact that grief in sound
pictures, and all tragedy for that matter, is difficult to
handle. Directors must use it sparingly and then with good
effect, or it will be only funny.

Did you see the film "Rango"? If you did, I am sure
that you liked the delightful naturalness of the introduction in which the man explained to the boy certain facts
about the orang-utan, or, as he called it, "Rango." Perhaps you enjoyed as I did the acting of Jackie Searle in the
picture "Tom Sawyer." He plays the part of the little
brother who is always making trouble, and is a rather hate-
ful little boy. An eighth-grade boy who saw the picture said
that either he would not like Jackie Searle in real life, or
Jackie Searle was a good actor. He meant that Jackie
Searle played his part so well that he thought perhaps Jackie
was only being natural. Of course, that is the highest compliment Jackie Searle could be paid—the compliment that
his acting appeared natural. Perhaps you also remember
the way Junior Durkin plays Huck Finn in the same picture.
I think you will agree that he was well cast.

An incident from the film "Morocco" has been mentioned in a motion-picture review by Robert Sherwood.
This incident shows how fine an interpretation a good actress can give to her rôle. The heroine, Amy Jolly (Marlene
Dietrich), is the guest of honor at a dinner party given by
her fiancé, La Bessière (Adolphe Menjou), to announce
their engagement. She has definitely ended her love affair
with Tom Brown (Gary Cooper), a private in the French
Foreign Legion, but, in the midst of a speech of congratu-
lation on the coming marriage, the marching music of the

Legion is heard in the distance. The drums and bugles grow louder and louder, until finally the girl jumps to her feet. As she turns toward the door, however, she catches and breaks the string of pearls which her fiancé had given her. But, unmindful of the scattering pearls, she hurries out of the house and, as in a dream, searches through the crowded streets for her lover.

Not a word is spoken by anyone during this incident; its only accompaniment is the distant war music. Dialogue at this point not only would have been useless but would have decidedly weakened the scene. The heroine's disregard of the broken string of pearls made any further explanation unnecessary, while the motion-picture director was able to bring out the full meaning of the incident by sharply focusing on it the attention of the audience.

Character Portrayal

If all of the elements of good acting have been consistently carried out, the final result is a satisfactory character portrayal. This means, then, that we must combine all these characteristics to make the character a believable one.

The film "Laughter" gave us an excellent example of character portrayal. Nancy Carroll tells her wealthy, middle-aged husband that she no longer loves him, that money is not sufficient for her happiness, but that she needs love and laughter. Her husband protests, but she leaves him. For a moment he stands quietly by his desk, fingering the tape from a near-by stock ticker. Then he drops his eyes and begins to read interestedly the quotations appearing on the tape. In a moment his thoughts are completely with the stock-market results, and he has entirely forgotten the previous incident. We see, therefore, that he is far more interested in business than he is in his wife.

LACK OF CONSISTENCY IN CHARACTERIZATION

A lack of consistency in characterization is sometimes found in motion pictures. In the picture "Office Wife," for example, the fiancé of the young woman is first shown as a rather delightful young man. Shortly afterward, however, with no warning, he develops into a selfish bore. If the rôle had been well developed, we should have seen this change coming gradually. There would have been hints of it from time to time. The sudden change caught the audience unprepared, and there is no doubt that they disliked it.

Another failure to develop a character consistently was illustrated in a picture in which Joan Crawford starred. First, we saw her as the heroine who is brought up as a harum-scarum on a South American ranch. A little later, however, she appeared in the drawing-room of a wealthy New York family. Her harum-scarum qualities were gone, and she spoke almost perfect English. Such things as these happen only in the movies, and they are not believable even there. Indeed, so frequently have we had acting of this type, and so many episodes have been shown in motion pictures which did not seem sensible, that the expression has arisen, "It could happen only in the movies."

THE STANDARD OF ENJOYMENT

Good acting gives two kinds of enjoyment. First, that which we secure at the time we see the picture. There is an emotional thrill in viewing an excellent performance, but there is another kind of enjoyment which comes from remembering the good acting which we have seen. In fact, it is highly possible that the best acting is likely to be remembered longest. For example, I can clearly remember now many scenes from "The Sin of Madelon Claudet," in which Helen Hayes starred. Perhaps most vivid was

her acting in the scene in which she was released from
prison. I shall probably never forget the skill with which
Ralph Morgan took the part of "Charlie" in "Strange
Interlude." Ruby Keeler appealed to me in the rôle which
she had in "42nd Street." Janet Gaynor was unforgettable
in "Street Angel." Junior Durkin did a splendid job playing the part of Huck Finn in the motion picture "Tom
Sawyer." Irene Dunne was excellent in "Cimarron" when
she spoke at the banquet given in her honor after her elec-
tion to Congress. Perhaps, then, we may say finally that
the best standard for good acting is the quality of the memory which it leaves.

Future Developments

Is motion-picture acting likely to improve as time goes
on? It likely will, although I do not believe anyone can
forecast with accuracy. Motion pictures were invented
only forty years ago, and in that time great progress has
been made—perhaps we can expect this progress to continue
at the same rate. As a matter of fact, however, a good deal
of this progress will depend upon you, not as an actor or
director, of course, but as a patron of acting—as one who
appreciates good acting and has an unfavorable attitude toward poor acting.

Motion-picture producers have, in certain instances, made
an attempt to substitute a pretty face and an attractive personality for good acting. While this may succeed for a short
time, it is a poor business method, since it causes many unfavorable opinions of motion pictures. This does not mean,
of course, that good acting is necessarily associated with
lack of personality or lack of beauty. It merely means that
personality and beauty are not substitutes for ability in
acting.

SUMMARY OF STANDARDS

Here are the standards which the writer sets up in this chapter for acting. If you do not agree with this set of standards, revise them to fit your own standards for a photoplay.

1. The actors and actresses should give the audience the feeling that they are real persons; they should seem natural.
2. The acting should give evidence that the part is well understood and is intelligently developed by the character.
3. A characterization should be carried out consistently throughout a picture.
4. A good story should be given a strong supporting cast, in addition to the usual one or two outstanding stars.
5. There should be no attempt to substitute good-looking heroes and heroines for actors of proved ability.
6. The make-up of a character should be such as to make him appear to be a real person.
7. Good acting gives evidence of skillful timing.
8. The effectiveness of the acting depends in large measure on the degree to which the settings, the plot, the photography, and other elements aid in creating the illusion of reality.

QUESTIONS FOR REVIEW

Here are some questions that members of the class may wish to ask themselves after they have seen a photoplay. Perhaps your group can find other questions which they wish to add, or they may wish to change this list.

1. Were the players well cast? Did they fit their rôles?
2. Was the supporting cast strong or weak?
3. What devices were used to introduce the various characters?
4. Did the characters seem natural in speech and manner?
5. Do you think that too much dependence was placed upon dialogue rather than upon photography? If so, indicate where.

6. Were the humorous parts of the play as well done as the serious parts?
7. How skillfully were strong emotions such as grief, anger, fear pictured? Were they overdone?
8. Were there examples of especially skillful use of make-up?
9. What were interesting bits of "business"?
10. Were the characterizations consistent?

CHAPTER VIII

PHOTOGRAPHY

To understand the art of the motion picture we must constantly realize that the motion picture is made with a camera. The camera is an all-seeing eye. It can record dramatic action from any point, below the action, above it, beside it, or at any angle. The camera eye can view the object at a distance, or can look at it closely. A great deal of the art of the motion picture lies in the skillful use of camera distance, that is, the distance of the camera from the object to be photographed, and camera angles, that is, the angle at which the action is photographed.

Photography, therefore, creates one of the most difficult problems in motion-picture criticism. Increased understanding of the skill of the cameraman will increase your appreciation of motion-picture production. One must not forget that a motion picture is something that has gone through a camera, something that has been improved by the skill of the cameraman and his director or harmed by the lack of it. As you gain an increased understanding of photography, you will increase your appreciation of motion pictures.

Principles of Photography

First of all, what are the principles of photography? Have you ever loaded a kodak? If you have, you know that you put a strip of celluloid film into your camera and adjust it so that when the lever is operated or the bulb is pressed, the film will be exposed. This permits the light coming from

121

the object to pass through the lens in such a way as to affect the chemicals on that strip of film. After you expose the entire roll you have it developed and printed. The process of development means that the strip is dipped in a chemical bath which brings out the picture in reverse; that is, white is black, and black is white. This makes the negative. The celluloid strips of film that you get back with your snapshots are negatives.

The negative is used to make the picture, the positive. This is done by holding the negative up against a piece of sensitive photograph paper and exposing it to the light. When this sensitive paper has been put into a chemical bath, the picture appears. It is dried, and then is ready to be returned to you. Here, then, are the steps in photography: expose to the light a bit of sensitized film, develop the film, print the picture from the negative, and develop the print. If you understand the simple applications of photography in the making of snapshots—that is, exposure, development, and printing—you will have little difficulty in understanding the making of motion pictures.

The Motion-Picture Camera

The diagram on page 123 shows the essential mechanism of a motion-picture camera without sound attachments. The roll at the upper right, marked "raw film," contains the film not yet exposed. A picture of this film, as used in standard motion-picture cameras, is shown in the lower left-hand corner of the diagram. The sprocket, so labeled, has gears that mesh with the holes in the film. When the crank, which is not shown here, is turned either electrically or by hand, the sprocket turns in such a way as to pull the film in the direction of the arrow. The film moves through the gate which is shown as a heavy black line.

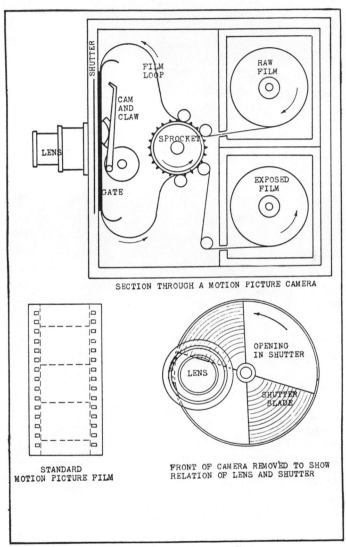

SECTION THROUGH A MOTION PICTURE CAMERA

STANDARD
MOTION PICTURE FILM

FRONT OF CAMERA REMOVED TO SHOW
RELATION OF LENS AND SHUTTER

Diagram of Motion-Picture Camera

When the film passes through this gate, it is exposed to the light which comes through the lens. The film moves through the gate in even jerks.

You know when you have exposed snapshot number one in your camera, you move the film slowly to snapshot number two. This is what happens in a motion-picture camera except of course that it is all done automatically and much more rapidly than you could possibly do it by hand in your still camera. In the case of the old silent motion pictures the camera made and the projector showed 16 separate pictures every second. In the sound pictures of today the normal rate is 24 pictures every second.

As soon as a single picture has been made, a claw pulls down another section of film. It does this over and over again 16 or 24 times a second while the camera is being operated, and the film pauses for a brief part of a second each time for the exposure to be made. After it is exposed, it keeps moving in the direction of the arrow and is rewound on the other reel at the bottom of the camera, marked "exposed film." The exposed film is later developed, and then printed.

What keeps the film from being exposed all the time? Why is it not exposed as it is pulled down by the claw? The reason it is not exposed at this time is that there is a rotating shutter between the lens and the gate (see the diagram in the lower right-hand corner) which keeps the film from the light, while it is being pulled down by this claw. The cam is the disk to which the claw is fastened. As the cam moves, the claw catches the film, pulls it down, disengages, catches it again, and so on. The film is exposed only when the claw is disengaged and moving up to pull down another section of film. Each section is known as a "frame."

When sound films are made, the camera must be inclosed

in such a way that it is soundproof. The camera covers are big unwieldy cases known as "blimps."

The lenses on these cameras are so arranged that they can be easily adjusted or changed. When a close-up is being taken, therefore, it may not be necessary to move the camera closer; the cameraman can merely change the lens. A cameraman may have a half dozen or more different lenses for his camera. Some of these will be short-focus, high-speed lenses, that can take pictures in poor light, sometimes even at night with bright street lights. Others will be long-focus lenses that bring distant objects closer, and he may have some of still longer focus that are known as telephoto lenses. With these he may photograph something across a wide street as large as though it were only eight or ten feet away. Or he may photograph a great mountain peak several miles away so large that it almost fills the picture. Long-focus lenses of the less extreme type are used generally for close-ups. Long-focus lenses are generally slower—that is, they need more light—than short-focus lenses. High-grade professional cameras have three and sometimes four lenses mounted on their turret fronts so that the cameraman may instantly change to any lens he wishes by a turn of his wrist.

A particular action may be photographed in a close-up, in a medium shot, and also at different angles. In this way the director can choose the shot which best fits his purpose and does not need to retake scenes. This method uses a great deal of film, however, and adds much to the cost of production.

Difference between Camera and Projector

You can get a good deal of assistance in learning about the camera by studying a motion-picture projector. Ar-

FAREWELL TO ARMS   *Paramount*

An extremely close close-up, in which the camera lens, representing Gary
Cooper's eyes, is only about two inches from Helen Hayes' face. This shot
presented a difficult lighting problem. Director Frank Borzage at left.

range with your neighborhood theater owner to view the projector and have it explained to you. Nearly every part of the projector is duplicated in the camera. Both the camera and the projector have lenses, film magazines, film-movement systems including intermittent mechanisms, and provisions for transmission of power to the various moving parts. But there the similarity ends. The camera takes pictures on highly light-sensitive negative and therefore is light-tight, except for the light admitted through the lens and shutter. The projector would be worthless without light and therefore a powerful light, usually a carbon arc, is a part of the projector.

The fundamental difference between a motion-picture camera and a motion-picture projector, of course, is that the camera takes pictures and the projector shows them. It is similar to the difference between a still camera which takes pictures and a stereopticon which projects pictures.

Types of "Shots"

When in this book we wish to emphasize particularly some point, we increase the size of the type, print it in capital letters, or put it in italics. Emphasis is also needed at certain points in motion pictures, and through the close-up, the medium shot, or long shot, the director is able to give varying types of emphasis or treatment to the material which appears later on the screen. These terms—close-up, medium shot, and long shot—usually mean rather specific things in reference to distance of the camera to the action. They may, however, refer to relative distances. The distance of the camera from a small vase in a close-up, medium shot, and long shot of it would, of course, differ greatly from the camera distances used in the same three shots of an automobile. In a well-directed and skillfully constructed motion picture these types of shots will be handled so artfully that you will hardly realize that varied camera distances are being used.

When Should the Close-Up Be Used?

When the director wishes to call your attention to something in the picture that does not loom large and may otherwise be unnoticed, he uses a close-up. This close-up may be of an object, such as a letter or a weapon, or of an actor's face. It is as if your seats in the theater were on a movable belt and you were being moved closer to or farther from the scene as the situation demanded.

What principle governs the use of close-ups—the close-up of a character's face, for instance? A close-up of an actor's face should be used only when necessary to see it at close range in order to understand his thought or action. If the same effect can be gained with a shot at a more natural distance, the close-up should be avoided.

The use of dialogue in pictures has changed in some degree the need for close-ups. When two persons are conversing, we often wish to see not only the speaker, but the person spoken to. Thus, the view often includes both persons, and the camera must be placed farther back in order to get both of them in the picture.

Here is what one star, Lee Tracy, thinks about close-ups, as pointed out in an article from the *New York Times* for May 24, 1933. He is speaking about a picture in which he appeared as the star.

> I didn't like "Clear All Wires" much. The director still had the old silent technique of close-ups. I never saw so many close-ups of Tracy in my life. There was no speed, no movement. . . . When we made "The Nuisance" I said to Jack Connelly, "Cut the close-ups. I'm not goodlooking and anyway they cut the action and speed."

The cameras are set for a close view.

MEDIUM AND LONG SHOTS

The most frequently used shot is the medium shot, which puts the spectator in the most natural position for watching the event unfold. Long shots are used when great perspective is desired or when atmosphere is sought. Excellent examples of skillful use of long shots are found in "Dracula," where the director, Tod Browning, puts his characters into huge rooms to show the smallness and insignificance of the human characters in the environment in which they had been placed. The same device is used in "Arrowsmith." We see Dr. Arrowsmith approaching the door of a huge building in which he is to work for a research institute. The scene is taken in a long shot, making Arrowsmith seem insignificant and puny and the institution large. The director's use of this shot may be interpreted as an attempt to help the audience understand Arrowsmith's position as he began his new duties.

In the making of films any scene from which the meaning can be obtained at normal range, that is, either a medium shot or a long shot, should be taken that way. The close-up should be used only where some of the meaning would be lost if the medium or long shot were used.

Why do I say this? The screen impressions should resemble our normal impressions. In life we get a close-up by moving nearer to a person. The movie, however, must bring the person's face closer to the camera. As a result, we frequently see a huge face covering the entire screen. When used too often and unnecessarily, such shots, I believe, tend to make us lose the illusion that the director is trying to build up. Do you agree?

The excessive use of the close-up may have other objections, some of which have been clearly stated by Mrs. Patterson:

In general, the transition from one camera distance to another follows the rules of social intercourse. People draw near to each other for intimate conversation; they draw apart to indicate lack of interest or anger. So in the continuity, when the action proceeds to a close-up, the spectators have an impression of drawing up their chairs; when the close-up breaks off suddenly into a long shot, they have a feeling of being rudely thrust back from the inner circle. There must be gradation in the use of camera distances.[1]

Moving Shots

Moving shots are difficult to make, and unless well done make the picture confusing and increase the difficulty of cutting. Further, the area which is lighted by a moving shot is greater, thereby increasing the difficulty of making the picture. The most important standard for moving shots is that they should appear so natural that the spectator is not conscious of them. In other words, the spectator's attention should not be drawn to the moving shot and away from the story. Better coöperation between the director and the head cameraman will eliminate many of these difficulties. It is said that the success of "Grand Hotel" was due in large measure to the excellent coöperation existing between Director Edmund Goulding and Cinematographer William Daniels.

Fade-In and Fade-Out

The fade-in, a device which you will see frequently in the motion pictures, is obtained by gradually increasing the amount of light until we have the scene in full light. It is similar in effect to the raising of the curtain in a stage production. A fade-out is obtained by gradually darkening the scene until it is black, and is similar to the lowering of the

[1] Patterson, Frances Taylor, *Scenario and Screen*, p. 95.

GRAND HOTEL   *Metro-Goldwyn-Mayer*

The use of a traveling crane makes it possible to obtain shots from a variety of angles and positions. Cameraman William Daniels is the man directly behind the camera while Director Edmund Goulding is the first man seated on the desk, to the left, in white trousers.

stage curtain. Fade-ins and fade-outs, therefore, are used to show a change from certain scenes to others. These changes will often be unnoticed, and rightly so, but one learns their true purpose when the director intentionally leaves them out. In "The Crowd" the director, King Vidor, wishes to show that his hero is living in the rush, roar, and hurly-burly of New York City. To secure this effect, he offers us a succession of short, typical views of the city, without fade-ins and fade-outs. The usual resting of the eye due to the gradual shifts from scene to scene is thus omitted, and the mental effect of this quick succession of images parallels the mental effect of New York on the stranger. Unless these flash shots are carefully used, however, the spectator is likely to become irritated by them.

THE DISSOLVE

In a dissolve, the scene that you see on the screen merges gradually with the next. Forceful results are secured by its wise use. In "Sin Takes a Holiday" the director wishes to show that his leading feminine character is enjoying the social whirl in a foreign capital. He does this cleverly by showing us a series of dissolves of whirling objects. A spinning roulette wheel dissolves into a swiftly moving automobile wheel, the hub cap of the auto replacing the center of the roulette wheel. This scene in turn merges into a view of a pair of skaters whirling in a circle about the same focus used in the two previous scenes.

Extremely long overlapping dissolves are used in the picture "Dishonored," directed by Josef von Sternberg. By means of these, the story flows smoothly since the decreasing interest in the scene just ending is carried into the next scene with mounting interest. In this film Von Sternberg also uses the dissolve as a recall device, giving an incident its full meaning by showing two scenes at the same time, the present one and an important previous one.

The heroine is a spy, and the plot hinges on a piece of music which she has composed, the notes of which contain a military code. She is captured and the music is destroyed, after having been played by an enemy officer. The heroine escapes, however, and later, on her own side of the lines, reconstructs the music from memory. She is shown playing the piano before a group of officers, now and then turning aside to jot down the notes. Upon this scene is briefly overlaid the previous scene in which she listens intently to the playing of the enemy officer. Although Von Sternberg sometimes uses this device unnecessarily, its use generally is not only desirable but highly effective.

Transition Devices

Have your themes or compositions ever been criticized by your teacher because they did not have good transition points? Do you jump too quickly from one paragraph to another? Transition points are equally important in motion pictures. Ends of chapters and transitional phrases like "on the other hand" and "at the same time," are needed in motion pictures as in writing. For example, the end of the scene is sometimes shown as a fade-out, and the beginning of the next scene by a fade-in. A shift of scene which does not break the action but carries it forward is shown by a dissolve. In other words, a fade-in or fade-out disconnects, but a dissolve connects.

I have said that a fade-out breaks the continuity—it distinguishes between different parts of the story. Able directors sometimes divide the story by other devices. For example, Welford Beaton in the *Hollywood Spectator*, March 11, 1933, says that "Rome Express" has only one fade-in, the one with which the picture begins, and only one fade-out, the one with which the picture ends. The director, Walter Ford, uses cuts to the exterior of the swiftly moving train as substitutes for fades.

Creativeness is especially needed in motion pictures in the transitions between different scenes. Sometimes we want to make a connecting link between the scenes, and here is an excellent opportunity for the director to use interesting and entertaining ideas. For example, the director of "The Infernal Machine" wishes to change the action from one deck of a boat in which we are looking directly into the mouth of a ventilator, to a deck below where people are dancing. He dissolves from a direct shot of the ventilator to a big bass horn. Here is a visual transition by means of similar appearance.

At other times we may have a transition where the scene fades out one object and fades in to another which may have similar motion. For example, a man may decide because of the hot weather to take a trip by plane instead of going by train. There is a fan whirling in front of him. A good transition shot would be to dissolve from a direct shot of this fan to the whirling propellor of the plane in which he is riding, or the transition might be made by means of the similar whirring sounds of the fan and the propellers.

UNUSUAL PHOTOGRAPHIC EFFECTS

In "Dr. Jekyll and Mr. Hyde" there was an interesting use of two different scenes on the same film. Hyde was shown walking in the park at the same time with a picture of his fiancée waiting for him in her home. This enabled the spectator to see two events which were occurring at the same time. Such attempts can best be judged by their effects.

The camera itself can be used to obtain remarkable effects.

Artistic camera work puts vigor into pictures which might otherwise be entirely commonplace. To appreciate the work of the cameraman and his instrument, ask yourself this question, "Where was the camera placed in order to secure this or that scene?"

By mounting the camera on a traveling crane (see page 135) it is possible to get a moving shot over the heads of a crowd, at a second-story window, and in other unusual positions. Such moving shots were frequently used in "All Quiet on the Western Front," a picture made by Universal Pictures Corporation. This company, like others, uses a special crane which makes breaks between certain scenes unnecessary, thus bringing about better continuity. Another device frequently used, and one which it will be interesting to look for, is that of trucking the camera past or along with the players. In this way, the audience can follow the action as the action itself moves along. Watch for wise and unwise uses of this device.

Illustrations of the use of interesting camera angles are given in the following incidents. In a card game in "The Street of Chance," a picture in which William Powell was starred, the camera was placed directly above the table and photographs taken from this angle. Usually pictures of a card game are taken as though the observer were sitting back of the player. Football huddles have also been photographed by pointing the camera up into the faces of the players or by taking the picture at a point directly above them. This type of shot should not be used merely to obtain a clever and different effect, but to give the audience a clearer view of some important action. Interesting effects are also procured by taking views with the camera lower than usual. This means that it sometimes must be tilted at a considerable angle when a person is being photographed. Such shots often heighten the illusion of the size of the object photographed. Would it make the object look smaller or larger? For example, in the French picture "Red Head" the hard-hearted mother is often photographed from an angle lower than the one usually used. This gave the spectator an indication of how the mother was seen by her little son.

After viewing a picture, one may sometimes enjoy thinking over ways in which the picture might have been improved. In "Rango," for instance, the shots of the fight between the water buffalo and the tiger could well have been closer. Apparently, the cameraman had taken all of the views above the action, but they would have been more effective at shorter range. This probably could have been done by use of a telephoto lens such as we have discussed, light permitting. We must remember that extremely long-focus lenses are not as fast as the shorter ones. However, to have "pulled up" the fights to larger size would have strengthened greatly the climax of the picture.

Filters and special lenses also are used to give certain effects. You all have seen shots in which there was an atmospheric softness that gave glamour to the scene. This effect is used especially in love scenes and other shots where the director wishes to give a romantic quality to the scene. It is done generally in one of two ways: either by shooting the scene with a special "soft-focus" lens, or by a special screen placed over the regular lens. Some filters darken the sky so that white clouds stand out in beautiful relief. See photograph on page 163. You may have seen scenes in foggy, steamy swamps in some pictures. These are made under ordinary conditions, probably in the studio, and shot through special fog filters.

If you have seen pictures in which scenes apparently were

taken through keyholes, portholes, field glasses, and so on, you will be interested to know that little metal masks with openings of the desired shapes are fitted into the camera which then actually takes the picture in the shape intended.

Lighting

Artificial lighting is used on all indoor sets, and unusual lighting adds much to the pictorial atmosphere. Exceedingly skillful effects were secured in the night scenes in "Tom Sawyer" and "Bulldog Drummond." In the picture "East Lynne," however, the scenes in the child's nursery, which were supposedly taken at night, were certainly overlighted. A baby ordinarily sleeps in a dark, or at least a semi-darkened room. On this occasion the room was as light as though it were day.

You will enjoy watching for special light effects. You probably have seen pictures in which a girl with light hair stood out in some scenes because her face seemed to be haloed with a flaming crown. This was done by playing a spotlight on her hair from a position above and facing the camera and following her with this light no matter where she moved. Lighting, too, can make a girl beautiful or unbelievably plain, and there are cases on record of film actresses and actors who have not succeeded because the light crews did not light them properly. This was in the early days, however, and lighting is as well organized now as every other phase of the film industry. Light is the stuff with which the photographer "paints" his pictures; his palette is a switchboard and battery of lights including spots, floods, carbon arcs, mercury vapor arcs, and mazda globes running into millions of watts. Lighting, of course, is under supervision of the director and the cameraman.

DR. JEKYLL AND MR. HYDE   *Paramount*

Note the contrast of light and shadow in this photograph.   Where was the camera placed to take this shot?

THE DIRECTOR AND THE CAMERAMAN

When the director and his cameraman sit down to plan and shoot a scene, it is much the same as an artist planning a painting—or a still photographer planning a picture. The artist has his model or models. He paints the picture on canvas with oil paints. The still photographer does much the same, except that he "paints" on a chemically coated plate with light and shadow—known to artists of brush and camera alike as *chiaroscuro.* Each artist must compose his picture. He must group his models and light them in such a way as to obtain good composition. He must have a pictorial sense.

The motion-picture director and cameraman must do all this and more. They have the same problems as the painter and still photographer, and must also plan the scene, not only so that the composition will be good, but so that it will continue to be good in spite of the movements of the actors. This, of course, is much more difficult than making a still picture. These men are artists in a new pictorial art which imposes new conditions and makes new demands.

CONCLUSION

We have not exhausted the possibilities in photography; inventive and creative directors will continue to produce effects of which the spectators have never dreamed. Did you ever think what possible difference on your attitude the moving of the camera right or left (called *panning* in the industry)[1] would make? You don't know what I mean, do you? Let Eric M. Knight, of the Philadelphia *Public Ledger* discuss this question for you. I include this quotation because long after you have read this book, and others like

---

[1] See definition in glossary.

it, these are going to be interesting photographic viewpoints
for you to think about.

Somewhat in the order of a teaser I chronicled that I knew
but six people in the world who had any idea why panning
right and panning left (or achieving the same result by intro-
ducing material onto the screen from the left or from the right)
produced such varying audience reactions.

Now we are seven. One reader begins to suspect the cause.

"I've been thinking about the different effects produced by
a right and left entry," writes K. K. Davis. "The eye moves
naturally from left to right with greater speed than from right
to left—so it picks up an entry from the right at once—as with
a flourish of trumpets; while an entry from the left can be
accomplished slyly and secretively before it is observed. Is
that the idea?"

Most certainly it seems to be the idea, and Miss Davis in-
dicates later in her letter why it is so. It all comes purely from
the fact that we start out as book readers in childhood. Our
eyes through the years learn to move from left to right—or to
state it another way, we become accustomed to all the abstract
shapes that make up the printed word moving into the range
of focus from the right.

Through constant repetition or habit we learn to accept any
entrance of material into the focal point from the right as normal
and graceful. From the left it comes awkwardly and, on the
screen, the eye must jump to meet it.

Miss Davis senses this for she continues:

"Carrying the idea to its logical conclusion, consider the
Oriental whose eyes move from the bottom to the top of the
page in reading. Must one conclude that the most effective
stage entrance for him would be from the flies. No—I'm just
being absurd."

It isn't absurd at all—providing Orientals do read from the
bottom up—I thought they read from the top down.

Whichever way it is, to them graceful entry of material
would be counter to the direction they read. And the big point
of cinema is that while the stage can't introduce its material
from above or below without great mechanical preparation, the

NIGHT FLIGHT   *Metro-Goldwyn-Mayer*

An interesting example of a close-up of a map.   Note the truck on which the camera is mounted.   Director Clarence Brown is standing at the left.

screen can do it as easily as not. Those who remember "The Front Page" will recall the unique effect produced by Lewis Milestone when he panned his cameras down successively on the faces of the reporters—bringing the material in from the bottom of his screen. It produced an eerie sort of jack-in-the-box sprightliness. I have not seen it essayed since.

At all events, no director seems willing to investigate all this. Some will use the effects as stunts, but few will attempt to find out exactly what the reaction is and, hence, exactly what legitimate use such refinements of camera work have outside their stunt value. When we use them correctly such things will stop being magic-lantern stunts and will become a real part of our cinema language.

SUMMARY OF STANDARDS

Here are the standards which the writer sets up in this chapter for photography. If you do not agree with this set of standards, revise them to fit your own standards for a photoplay.

1. Variations from the normal camera angle (four feet, six inches above the floor) should not be made except to obtain a necessary effect.
2. Most of the scenes in a picture should be medium shots.
3. The chief value of the long shot is to give the setting of an event.
4. The chief purpose of the close-up is to call your attention to some otherwise unnoticed object, person, or action.
5. The good director will use a variety of shots—long, medium, and close-up.
6. The use of double exposure (two pictures one on top of the other) is especially valuable in showing what a character is thinking about.
7. A "flash" shot should be used to give the spectator a quick mental image of a face or some object.
8. The fade-in and fade-out may logically be used where there is

a change or disconnection in the story. The dissolve is valuable for connecting scenes without interrupting the flow of the story.

9. A picture should usually be so lighted as to give natural effects.

QUESTIONS FOR REVIEW

Here are some questions that members of the class may wish to ask themselves after they have seen a photoplay. Perhaps your group can find other questions which they wish to add, or they may wish to change this list.

1. Was there satisfactory use of long shots? Medium shots? Close-ups? If not, how might the play have been improved?
2. What scenes were photographed from unusual camera angles? Were they necessary? Were they successful?
3. Can you give any examples of especially skillful or unskillful use of the close-up? Long shot? Double exposure? Flash shots? Out-of-focus shots? Fade-ins? Fade-outs? Panoramas? Trucking-up shots? Dissolves?
4. What examples did you notice of skillful and unskillful uses of lighting?
5. Were there examples of beautiful photography? If so, was the beautiful photography appropriate to the picture?

CHAPTER IX

SETTINGS

The Function of Settings

THE success of any motion picture depends a great deal on the way the settings have been arranged to tell their story. Settings are the frame of a picture. That frame must not be so garish or so unusual that attention is attracted from the picture itself. Good settings, therefore, will not shout at you; they will merely whisper. If well planned, they never force themselves into the scene in such a way that attention is drawn away from the action on the screen. Good settings will create the proper mood or atmosphere. Each picture, therefore, demands different treatment as far as settings are concerned, since the mood or atmosphere will vary.

This can be easily illustrated by referring to a specific story. Let's suppose now that you are to be the art director of "The Fall of the House of Usher," by Edgar Allan Poe. Here is the opening paragraph, which illustrates the background of this story:

During the whole of a dull, dark, and soundless day in the autumn of the year, when the clouds hung oppressively low in the heavens, I had been passing alone, on horseback, through a singularly dreary track of country; and at length found myself, as the shades of the evening drew on, within view of the melancholy House of Usher. I know not how it was—but, with the first glimpse of the building, a sense of insufferable gloom pervaded my spirit. I say insufferable; for the feeling was unrelieved by any of that half-pleasurable, because poetic, sentiment with which the mind usually receives even the sternest

151

natural images of the desolate or terrible. I looked upon the scene before me—upon the mere house, and the simple landscape features of the domain, upon the bleak walls, upon the vacant eye-like windows, upon a few rank sedges, and upon a few white trunks of decayed trees, with an utter depression of soul which I can compare to no earthly sensation more properly than to the after-dream of the reveller upon opium: the bitter lapse into every-day life, the hideous dropping off of the veil. It was possible, I reflected, that a mere different arrangement of the particulars of the scene, of the details of the picture, would be sufficient to modify, or perhaps to annihilate, its capacity for sorrowful impression; and, acting upon this idea, I reined my horse to the precipitous brink of a black and lurid tarn that lay in unruffled lustre by the dwelling, and gazed down—but with a shudder even more thrilling than before— upon the remodelled and inverted images of the grey sedge, and the ghastly tree-stems, and the vacant and eye-like windows.

With what type of setting will you open the picture? Will it be on a bright, sunshiny day, or will you try to create the effect of dullness, drabness, and darkness? Will you have the horseman riding on a white horse? Will you use a white house with green shutters for the "melancholy House of Usher"? Just what will you do to create in the setting a "sense of insufferable gloom"?

This opening illustration is probably complete enough to give you the notion that settings are far more important than we realize in giving the audience the right mental setting for what is to follow. I should like to suggest that sometime you stay through the second showing of a picture that you have enjoyed and then note the great detail which the art director has carried out in his settings. It will add enjoyment to your picture-going.

W. C. Menzies, a motion-picture director, explains here just how the art director and the cameraman can help a story by giving it the proper setting:

The art director and the cameraman, with their many mechanical and technical resources, can do a great deal to add punch to the action as planned by the director. For example, if the mood of the scene calls for violence and melodramatic action, the arrangement of the principal lines of the composition would be very extreme, with many straight lines and extreme angles. The point of view would be extreme, either very low or very high. The lens employed might be a wide angled one, such as a twenty-five millimeter lens which violates the perspective and gives depth and vividness to the scene. The values or masses could be simple and mostly in a low key, with violent highlights.

In a scene such as the one to which I have just referred, when the tempo of the action is very fast, there are usually rapidly changing compositions of figures and shadows. For idyllic love scenes, or scenes demanding beauty, the values and forms are usually softer, the lens is diffused and the grouping and dressing graceful and lyrical. In the case of pageantry such things as scale and pattern, figures, rich trappings against a high wall, through a huge arc, are demanded. In comedy scenes the composition may be almost in the mode of caricature. In tragedy or pathos, or any scene photographed in a low key, the setting is often designed with a low ceiling, giving a feeling of depression.[1]

We see, therefore, that there is need for a great deal of coöperation between the scenic artist and the technical department in order that they may determine the values which are to be emphasized and the atmosphere to be created. The artist may prepare sketches to indicate in general the effects he is trying to secure. Sometimes models of the sets will be prepared. It will be necessary to determine whether to build a set completely, whether to make it in miniature, or whether to use certain paintings on glass which will give the same effects.

[1] "The Artistic Phases of Picture Making," Part III, *A Motion Picture Study Program*, pp. 11–12.

The Development of Settings

The history of the development of appropriate settings is an interesting and novel story. W. C. Menzies has also told of it. He points out first of all the crudity of early settings:

In the earliest pictures, little, if any, attention was given to background. These were the novelty days, when the mere seeking of movement on the screen was sufficient to satisfy the public. The background was whatever happened to be behind the object or person photographed. The next step was a sort of travelogue background, using natural settings. As the pictures were done with a limited personnel, and in a short time, the backgrounds were not very carefully selected. In fact, it was quite usual for a company to go into the country in the morning with a camera, a couple of horses and an actor or two, and return in the evening with an epic of the period.

With the coming of stories demanding interiors the first sets had to be devised. These were originally, either a borrowed stage set, or a painted canvas backing. All the wall furniture, such as bookcases, pictures, and so forth, was painted on a flat surface. Even vases with flowers, and chairs against the wall were painted, the only objects not being painted being those in the center of the room in actual use in the action. The company making the picture usually painted a trademark in a conspicuous place on the wall. For instance, Pathe used its rooster trademark in this way.

The sets were made of light framework and canvas, so that when an actor entered and closed the door the whole room, including the painted furniture, would shake. Usually, these sets were set up outside, and were lit by sunlight, giving a peculiar outside effect to a supposed interior. In addition the cameraman often had to pan up the camera to avoid showing the grass or dirt floor, and if a wind happened to be blowing, the actor almost had to hold on to his hat to keep it from blowing out of the scene. These early sets were designed principally by scenic artists or head carpenters, and often the plan or sketch was drawn on an old envelope or the stage floor. In fact, an early

TOM SAWYER

A careful study of this perfect reproduction of an old-fashioned kitchen will convince you that the art director plays an important part in the making of a motion picture.

designer of my acquaintance used to design his sets on the palm of his hand if nothing else happened to be handy. These early sets merely filled the requirements of entrance and exit, but in some cases they were surprisingly well done. The advent of the open stage did not help matters much, for, though the lighting was controlled by diffusers, or large overhead awnings, which could be rolled back and forth, the lighting throughout the scene would be continually changing with the movement of the sun.

But the public became more critical. They wanted more reality in their settings. They wanted more artistic settings.

As lighting equipment developed, the glass stage was abolished or darkened in, and all lighting was artificially created. At this time, artists and architects began to take a hand in designing sets. Texture, effects and composition began to be considered, and efforts were made to please the newly awakened taste of the public, which was growing more discriminating, now that the first novelty of the first motion picture had worn off. Gradually through the efforts of illustrators, painters, stage designers, architects, and commercial artists—all of whom had tried their hand at movie design—the set of the present day was evolved.

The set of today is neither a purely architectural nor a purely artistic product. It is an ingenious combination of art, architecture, dramatic knowledge, engineering, and craftsmanship. It combines in just the right proportions theatrical license with the reality of good architectural pattern. Simplicity and restraint are its chief characteristics. Simplicity is absolutely necessary for the audience must be able to grasp the whole scene and its meaning at a glance.

. . . .

So you see the motion-picture technician must have great ingenuity. He must have a knowledge of architecture of all periods and nationalities. He must be able to picturize and make interesting, a tenement or a prison. He must be a cartoonist, a costumer, a marine painter, a designer of ships, an interior decorator, a landscape painter, a dramatist, an inventor, an historical, and now, an acoustical expert—in fact, a "Jack-of-all-trades."

ILLUSTRATIONS OF SKILLFUL SETTINGS

Following are some examples of the able use of settings. In "Tom Sawyer" the events are laid in the year 1850. The scenes put us at once into the atmosphere of that period —the broad stretch of the Mississippi River, the paddle-wheel steamboat, the general store handling all kinds of goods, the fashions of the day—all these together make a background which effectively creates the proper rea?tion in the one who views the motion picture.

"Abraham Lincoln" also illustrates an interesting and successful use of settings. The opening scenes of the play show the cruelty and brutality of the slave trade, and fill us with indignation like that with which Lincoln was inflamed. Later in the film, we see the drab, unfavorable conditions under which Lincoln was born. A moving camera shot shows a stretch of bleak, bare tree stumps; the howling of the wind is heard; finally the camera stops before the rude cabin which was the birthplace of Abraham Lincoln. The audience has thus been properly prepared for the theme of the play, that out of a bleak and unkindly environment there comes a man who is to relieve the sufferings of a race. This introduction shows the rare skill with which the director, David Wark Griffith, has prepared his audience emotionally for the scenes which are to follow.

The success of the motion picture "Dracula" can be credited in large part to the settings which are used in the picture. Surely, if vampires lived, they would prefer for a home an old castle such as the one shown in this picture. The effectiveness of the sets of "State Fair" has already been commented upon.

UNDER THE TONTO RIM   *Paramount*
This shows the company on location.

THE USE OF OUTDOOR SETTINGS

W. C. Menzies points out further that:

As much as is possible, now-a-days, everything is shot on the lot. Forests, ships, country lanes, mountains, canals, and all, are built up and tricked. So that what, on the screen, may cover miles of ground, in reality, only occupies a few acres of back lot, or a few hundred square feet of stage.

However, there are times when the breadth of action makes it necessary to secure outdoor shots. The area around Hollywood is particularly well suited to the construction of outdoor motion pictures, since it has such a wide variety of scenery. It is possible to go quickly from semi-tropical scenes to scenes of snow and ice.

For example, one of the locations used in recent talking picture productions is the "Lake Sherwood" region or the old Canterbury Ranch. It has an area of about eight thousand acres and is only fifty miles from Hollywood. Douglas Fairbanks used it for the forest scenes for his silent picture "Robin Hood." It was also recently used for water scenes in "Tarzan, the Ape Man," mountain scenes in "Private Lives," the dueling scene from Buster Keaton's "The Passionate Plumber," and the lake scenes in "Emma." Further, there is a huge pasture on this ranch which was the locale for the Indian fight in "The Great Meadow." The Santa Monica Canyon, a few miles from Hollywood, was the site of a Cuban village constructed for use in "The Cuban Love Song."

A number of motion pictures call for ocean and waterfront backgrounds. Small coves near Laguna are used for this purpose. The Los Angeles city reservoir, known as Lake Franklin, is often used for scenic backgrounds. Beautiful willow trees ornament its banks, and the fishing scenes in "Susan Lenox" were photographed there, as well as the ferry-boat scene in "Private Lives." This spot is especially adapted for motion pictures since it is not within the route followed by passenger airplanes, and there is no public automobile road within miles.

These facts must now be considered in choosing outdoor settings, since the sound would be easily picked up by the sensitive microphones.   Indeed, this nearness to public highways has made it necessary to abandon some of the favorite spots for the making of motion pictures.   For example, a woodland spot near Glendale—a few miles north of Hollywood—was commonly used in the making of silent motion pictures.   It has a running stream, beautiful trees, a variety of flowers, is only twenty minutes from some of the studios, and appears to be in the heart of the mountains.   But, unfortunately, sound films cannot be taken here since it is near a street car line and is only a few feet from the heavily traveled main highway.   The old Providencia ranch, north of Hollywood near Burbank, which was used for many of the scenes of Rudolph Valentino's "Blood and Sand" and many of the scenes for "The Covered Wagon," is seldom used now because it is too near some of the big airplane routes.[1]

Standards for Judging Settings

The best standard by which to judge a setting is, of course, the feeling of reality which it gives you. When you can easily tell that a jungle setting has been made in a studio the effect of the whole picture is spoiled for you, because you think, "Oh, it's all a fake." Even if a jungle setting is made in the studio, it should be so well done that you always think that the setting is real.

[1] Adapted from an article in the *New York Times*, April 24, 1932, p. 5.

Metro-Goldwyn-Mayer

WHITE SHADOWS IN THE SOUTH SEAS

The cameraman, Bob Roberts, was responsible for securing this photograph of tropical beauty.

However, this does not mean that the setting will be exactly as it would be in real life. It is the illusion of reality for which the artist is striving; therefore, to the facts of life must be added the imagination of the scenic artist who develops the set. It is true that the modern settings are realistic. In other words, they do look as the scene does in real life. However, in certain of the foreign pictures, notably "The Cabinet of Dr. Caligari," impressionistic or symbolic effects were used. The crazy angles and unreal settings conveyed to the audience the element of horror and supernaturalism which was the keynote of the film. Of course, here we had an abnormal person, and we would expect to see abnormal settings.

We must remember, however, that the same standard of truthfulness applies not only to settings of pictures taken in Africa, but also to settings of pictures in this country. Settings should, therefore, be judged by their appropriateness, that is, by the way in which they fit the characters in the play. Many settings are inappropriate as the living quarters of the characters impersonated; for example, a $20-a-week clerk sometimes is shown living in an apartment which he could not possibly afford on that income, and a shopgirl will show taste in the selection and furnishing of an apartment that would do credit to an interior decorator. Good directors do not make this mistake.

According to Cedric Gibbons, art director for Metro-Goldwyn-Mayer, in designing a set, if it is a home, the artist must bear in mind the type of person who is going to live in that home. The naïve, unsophisticated girl must not be photographed against a smartly decorated, modernistic background. Settings must, therefore, be judged by their appropriateness. Mr. Gibbons says:

> A motion-picture set . . . should be primarily a background for the action that takes place in it and the personalities who live in it.
>
> Good motion-picture settings not only express what is going to happen on those sets, but are designed as suitable backgrounds for the personalities of the players. Anyone passing by and seeing the various sets can tell about what types of scenes are to be played in them, as well as what types of people will enact them.[1]

Another standard of judgment is the historical accuracy of the settings. Here, of course, only the worst errors can be noted by those who know little about the history of the period shown. These mistakes do occur, however, and one writer says that the criticism of the public is the only influence which will keep some directors from making such blunders, for

> if it were not for these same observing and critical persons, Heaven knows to what lengths some directors would go in their indifference to custom, traditions, consistency and good taste, through their scorn of things with which they are not personally familiar.[2]

Another important standard for settings is variety. It is possible, of course, that they might be accurate, that they might be appropriate, but that they would be either too few, or too much the same throughout the picture. The picture "Topaze" was weakened for me somewhat because of the fact that, as I remember it now, there were only a few sets. Variety, of course, is not only variety within a picture itself, but variety from picture to picture. There is a great deal of sameness in the settings which we find in motion pictures. The sophisticated heroine nearly always

[1] Gibbons, Cedric, "Every Home's a Stage," *Ladies' Home Journal*, July, 1933, pp. 25 and 77.
[2] Smith, H. M. K., "Mistakes That Directors Make," *New York Times*, November 24, 1929.

BEN HUR   *Metro-Goldwyn-Mayer*
    This garden scene of rare beauty increased the enjoyment of the spectators
of this film.

lives in a modernistically decorated home, and how similar these homes all are! This similarity is inexcusable because you know from experience that no two of your friends— even though they may be on the same financial level—have homes as similar in decoration as are most of these settings. Why, then, should a good director feel that he must place against an identical background every character belonging to a certain social class?

SUMMARY OF STANDARDS

Here are the standards which the writer sets up in this chapter for settings. If you do not agree with this set of standards, revise them to fit your own standards for a photoplay.

1. In a serious picture the settings should provide enough atmosphere to give the story the appearance of reality.
2. A setting must be simple enough for the audience quickly to grasp the whole scene and its meaning.
3. It makes no difference if a setting is artificial, as long as it seems real.
4. Settings in an historical picture should be an accurate representation of the period in which the story takes place.
5. A setting should not take the attention of the audience away from important action.
6. The costuming should contribute to the atmosphere of the play.

QUESTIONS FOR REVIEW

Here are some questions which members of the class may wish to ask themselves after they have seen a photoplay. Perhaps the students in your group can find other questions which they wish to add, or they may wish to change this list.

1. Did the settings help or hinder in creating a feeling of reality?
2. Were any of the settings so unusual that they took the attention of the audience away from important action?
3. Were the settings simple enough for the audience to grasp quickly the whole scene and its meaning?
4. Was it possible to tell that some of the scenes were not real, but were merely movie sets? If so, is this undesirable?
5. Did you notice any errors in the historical settings? If so, what were they?
6. Would the picture have been improved if a greater variety of sets had been used?
7. When scenes were laid in industrial, commercial, or agricultural settings, was there an attempt made to give the audience a great deal of insight into life in these fields? If not, could it have been done?
8. Did the costuming lend reality to the picture? How?

CHAPTER X

SOUND AND MUSIC

The Development of Sound

MANY of you can remember when talking pictures first appeared. The first pictures of this type were shown in 1926, and by 1929 most of the larger theaters had been equipped and were using sound pictures almost entirely. According to the *Motion Picture Herald*, 13,091 of the 13,247 motion-picture theaters operating at the end of 1932 in the United States were wired for sound. Perhaps you wonder why sound motion pictures did not come before. As a matter of fact, the idea was one that had occurred to the early inventors of the motion picture, but the electrical synchronization which we now have was not then developed. In 1916, Epes Winthrop Sargent said:

> Although it is not to be supposed that talking pictures will ever replace the silent drama, since it merely gives back a poor travesty on the speaking stage, and the injection of dialogue defeats the end of the motion picture, it is only a question of time when the perfection of the device will bring it forward as a form of entertainment. The chief value of a talking picture will lie in its ability to reproduce the action and support the phonograph record. It will be possible to both see and hear the operatic and dramatic star.[1]

Sound effects can be obtained in two ways. One is by means of a sound record on a disk like a phonograph record. This was demonstrated for the first time in 1926 under the name "Vitaphone." The other method of sound reproduc-

[1] *Techniques of the Photoplay*, p. 302.

171

tion is on the film itself. The use of the sound track on the film reduces the size of the picture, so today the motion picture thrown on the screen is smaller in size than it was before the development of motion pictures with sound. Every major company now uses the sound-on-film method.

How Much Dialogue?

With new inventions and improvements there was a period of fumbling before the technicians and actors learned how to use sound and speech in motion pictures. May I point out some of these difficulties?

The chief purpose of dialogue and sound in a play is to create the illusion of reality. Good dialogue intensifies and promotes the action of the play. You should judge its success, then, with this standard in mind.

Stage plays sometimes suffer from too much dialogue, but one gets relief through looking around the theater, through watching the different characters, and through the enjoyment of the color and movement which one usually sees on the stage. Even here, however, one frequently attends a play which talks itself to death; for example, if you have seen George Bernard Shaw's "The Apple Cart," you will know what I mean. The speeches are so long that most people tire of hearing them; reading them is probably more satisfactory. Since stage plays sometimes suffer because of excessive dialogue, the motion picture, which ought to lean more heavily on photography than on dialogue, should guard against falling into this error. Welford Beaton does not object to the use of sound in a motion picture, but says in *Know Your Movies*, pp. 98–99:

> No sound that is not of itself entertaining has a legitimate place on the screen. Nothing that is real belongs in an art of the illusion of reality, but we can stretch that point now and

then and bring to picture houses such real sounds as are so
pleasant in themselves that they glide into the dreams that we
are weaving with the material supplied us on the screen—the
song of a bird, the ripple of a stream, a cow-bell tinkling in a
meadow; even the sustained low note of a locomotive whistle
as a train glides through the mountains a long way off. For
dramatic effect, too, actual sound sometimes can be effective,
but such instances are rare, and the sound is harmful when in-
dulged in too freely.

Nothing that can be left to the imagination should be included in a motion picture. When we watch a door slam our
imaginations supply the noise; when we see a tray of dishes fall
it is not necessary to tell us that it makes a noise. The whole
reason for the prosperity and immense importance of the film
industry might be said to be wrapped up in the fact that it
could show us a tray of dishes falling without jangling our nerves
with the resultant noise—and now the industry goes to great
pains to gather in the noise and assail our ears with it.

The major standard set up by Beaton is that the sound or
dialogue must not interrupt the story. Interruptions stop
the flow of motion. They sidetrack us. They lower the interest. Songs, dialogue, speeches, and noises may be included as long as they are an important part of the story,
but no sound that is likely to interrupt, to break one's continued thinking about the play, should be included.

How can one tell whether there is too much dialogue,
too much music? I have noticed that persons who are accustomed to seeing stage performances do not object so
strongly to excessive dialogue as do those who are more
accustomed to viewing motion pictures. A number of my
friends, for example, thought that "Topaze" was excellent.
The majority of these persons, however, attend motion
pictures only rarely and view legitimate stage productions
frequently. I was disappointed in "Topaze" not because
John Barrymore's acting was poor or because the plot it-

self was weak, but because the use of the camera in telling the story was not satisfactory. Further, it appeared to put an extreme emphasis on dialogue.

One test of whether or not the full possibilities of the camera were utilized is to turn your eyes away from the screen and see whether the story is carried by the dialogue. If the dialogue alone is sufficient to carry the story, it is my belief that the picture is far weaker than if the camera had been used to tell what was happening. If dialogue without sight carries the play, why not listen to it over the radio?

Microphones Aren't Human

Perhaps the most common mistake made in the use of sound is the attempt *exactly* to reproduce all sounds as they occur in real life. The objection to this use of sound is an important one. The human ear does not hear all the sounds that a microphone picks up. The microphone cannot determine the effect the sound is going to have on a person. As a matter of fact there are sounds about us all the time, but frequently we do not hear them because we are not paying any attention to them. By listening carefully I can hear a typewriter clacking away in the next room. If some one were taking a motion picture of a man at work at his desk, would they include this sound? Probably not, unless they were trying to show that this person was distracted and unable to work, since it is only under such circumstances that he would hear such sounds.

Here are some other examples. An elevated train rushing past the window of a second-story flat would hardly be heard by a pair of lovers seated in a living room. However, the sound of that same elevated would be a distracting roar to a nerve-racked woman who hated to live in such an environment.

(Sounds of the elevated, by the way, were made for one picture by running roller skates around large iron plates. This gave the right click and needed only to be timed with the speed of the train on the screen.)

A clock ticking in a room would not be heard by a convict who was plotting a robbery. However, a clock ticking in his death cell would reach abnormal proportions. In other words, the director of a picture must realize that the microphone must hear only those sounds which have value in creating the illusion of reality. Sometimes sounds are dramatic and have value in aiding the development of the motion picture. At other times they are valueless and if introduced would only be a distraction from the major theme of the play.

Should we always hear an automobile as it grinds into second gear? Many persons would say no. In other words, we are merely asking that the microphone, like the camera, be selective and pick out for hearing only those sounds which will add to the dramatic value of the scene.

Skillful use of sound is illustrated in the motion picture "Monte Carlo." A shot of the driving wheels of a locomotive is presented, accompanied by the usual rushing and roaring sounds, with an occasional blast of the train whistle. Gradually, however, there is interwoven a thread of music, using in its rhythm the clicking of the rails, the blast of the whistle, and the other train sounds. Slowly the music swells in volume till it provides an accompaniment to a song.

The Use of Music in Films

There are two types of use of music in films. One is that in which the music accompanies the action, whether it be from an instrument which has a place in the film, as a piano or phonograph or radio, and the other is music from a source which one is unable to see on the screen.

Music in motion pictures ought to help develop the mood of the picture. It ought not to act as an interruption, but should heighten and intensify the emotion of the spectator. It should not be used in an attempt to induce emotions and feelings in the audience when the full possibilities of the picture itself have not been utilized in this direction. In other words, the music must be an aid to the picture itself and not attempt to take its place. It must supplement but not supplant.

Music, of course, was long used with the silent film. Indeed, there were some compositions which were specially prepared for use with silent films. Many a love scene has taken place to the accompaniment of "Hearts and Flowers"—so many, that today it is used only as a burlesque.

The Work of the Director of Music

The director of music must either compose or select a musical accompaniment which will create the desired atmosphere. Erno Rapée, well-known musical authority, sets up this prescription for synchronizing pictures: "First," he says, "determine the geographical and national atmosphere of the picture. Then embody every important character with a theme."[1] How will the director know what that atmosphere should be? He can obtain this understanding only by working with the director of the picture. If this is not done, the music and the picture itself are likely to be poorly coördinated.

In some cases music already composed can be selected to create that atmosphere. If music already composed is

[1] Arvey, Verna, "Present Day Musical Films and How They Are Made Possible," *The Etude*, January, 1931, pp. 16–17 and 61 and 72.

used, care must be taken so that it does not set up associations in the mind of the hearer that are unrelated to the theme of the picture. Music, then, like sound, must follow certain standards.

An extremely important standard for the music used is that it show good taste and discriminating judgment. In other words, it ought to be good music. Many believe that this standard is not being adequately met in motion pictures. For example, a famous composer, Charles Wakefield Cadman, said in the *Music World* of September, 1930: "The musical taste of most of the studios is very low, and it has not improved one whit since music for sound pictures came in. I feel that we had better music with the old silents than we do right now."

SUMMARY OF STANDARDS

1. The sound or dialogue must not interrupt the flow of the story.
2. The story ought to be told primarily by the camera and not by dialogue.
3. Only those sounds should be included in the picture which have dramatic value.
4. The purpose of music is to help develop the mood or atmosphere of the picture.

PROBLEMS AND ACTIVITIES

1. Do people under strong emotion use long or short sentences? What evidence have you for your statement?
2. Do you prefer action to talk in a motion picture? Why?
3. What difference, if any, does it make how much the characters talk and how often they talk?
4. Write a review of the dialogue and sound effects of a motion picture, bearing these questions in mind:
   a. Did the dialogue intensify and promote the action of the play? Give some examples.

 b. Did it appeal to you as real?

 c. Were there any places where action might have been substituted for dialogue with better effect?

 d. What unusual sound effects did you notice? Unnecessary ones?

 e. How was music used as a sound effect, if at all? Suggest possible changes in the music used.

 f. Was any of the dialogue so long as to be boring? How could this have been remedied?

 g. If you saw Frederic March in "Dr. Jekyll and Mr. Hyde," tell your classmates what you thought of the sound effects used when Dr. Jekyll was changing over to Mr. Hyde.

CHAPTER XI

DIRECTION

The Importance of the Director

Do you think that Helen Hayes and Norma Shearer are great actresses? If you do, can you tell me who directed their latest pictures? If you are unable to answer this question, then your understanding of motion pictures is quite elementary, because one of the most important persons in the making of a motion picture is the director. Now I am going to try a simple test on you. Get paper and pencil and see whether you can match the names of the directors, whose photographs appear on pages 182–183, with the films which they directed in the following list:

1. "Farewell to Arms"
2. "Street Scene"
3. "Thunder over Mexico"
4. "A Nous la Liberté"
5. "Dishonored"
6. "Oliver Twist"
7. "City Lights"
8. "Broken Lullaby"
9. "Dirigible"
10. "Abraham Lincoln"

If you are like most high-school students and most adults to whom I have put this problem, you have not succeeded well at this task. The fact that you know much about motion-picture stars and but little about motion-picture directors shows that you have not thought seriously about the different phases of motion pictures.

As a matter of fact, a knowledge of a star's director is more important to you from the standpoint of an understanding of motion pictures than is a knowledge of what the star wears in the afternoon, whether she likes buttered toast, the number of hounds she has around her place, and the other things that motion-picture magazines publish about stars. I do not mean that directors are all-important and that the stars are but their puppets and unimportant. Far from it. I do mean that making motion pictures is a coöperative enterprise in which stars, directors, other members of the cast, and technicians must share honors.

You may be interested in knowing that formerly the *Film Daily*, a trade magazine, was accustomed to poll about three hundred motion-picture critics and ask them to name the best directors of that year. Although this has not been done for the past two years, the directors chosen for this honor in 1930–31 and the pictures which they directed are:

Lewis Milestone
   "All Quiet on the West-
   ern Front"
   "The Front Page"
Wesley Ruggles
   "The Sea Bat"
   "Cimarron"
George Hill
   "The Big House"
   "Min and Bill"
Josef von Sternberg
   "The Blue Angel"
   "Morocco"
D. W. Griffith
   "Abraham Lincoln"
Howard Hawks
   "The Criminal Code"
   "The Dawn Patrol"

Robert Z. Leonard
   "The Divorcee"
   "In Gay Madrid"
   "Let Us Be Gay"
   "Bachelor Father"
   "It's a Wise Child"
John Cromwell
   "The Big Pond"
   "For the Defense"
   "Tom Sawyer"
   "Scandal Sheet"
   "Unfaithful"
Charles Chaplin
   "City Lights"
Howard Hughes
   "Hell's Angels"

Those named on the honor roll were:

Alfred E. Green, Edward H. Griffith, Clarence Brown, Ernst Lubitsch, George Fitzmaurice, Robert Milton, Mervyn LeRoy, Raoul Walsh, Lloyd Bacon, Harry D'Arrast, John Blystone,

Courtesy of Motion-Picture Herald

A GROUP OF OUTSTANDING

1. Frank Borzage;   2. Herbert Brenon;   3. Frank Capra;   4. Charles Chaplin; 5. René Clair; 6. Cecil B. De Mille.

Courtesy of Motion-Picture Herald

MOTION-PICTURE DIRECTORS

1. Sergei Eisenstein; 2. D. W. Griffith; 3. Ernst Lubitsch; 4. Lewis Milestone; 5. King Vidor; 6. Josef von Sternberg.

Harry Beaumont, Edmund Goulding, Victor Fleming, Lionel
Barrymore, Ernest B. Schoedsack, and Tod Browning.

What does a motion-picture director do? The director is
the man in the studio who superintends the making of the
motion picture. He is responsible for its final form, and its
effectiveness depends on his ability. It is, therefore, important that you become acquainted with the work of the ablest
directors, because this information will often enable you to
make a better selection of films to attend. For example, you
may be sure that if you go to see a picture directed by King
Vidor or Ernst Lubitsch you are certain not to be wholly
disappointed, because you will always have the opportunity
of viewing artistic work.

Some Outstanding Directors and Their Work

Let us pause for a moment to discuss the work of different directors. I should like to point out to you the various
ways in which each director does his work, but that, of
course, is impossible. Some writers have attempted to say
that Von Sternberg does this, Vidor does that, and Lubitsch
does something else, but it is doubtful whether any except
a few experts would be able to pick the director of a picture
without previously knowing who made it. Some people may
be able to do this, but the distinguishing characteristics are
so few that it would be difficult. It is true, of course, that
there are real differences among the work of directors, but
whenever a director does an unusual piece of work, his
methods soon become common property. Thus a method of
motion-picture making that is originated by one director
will soon be used by others.

Perhaps the greatest name in motion-picture direction is
that of David Wark Griffith, who has to his credit such productions as "Intolerance," "Broken Blossoms," "Hearts of

the World," "Dream Street," "Orphans of the Storm," "Way Down East," "Abraham Lincoln," and "The Birth of a Nation," perhaps his greatest picture. Griffith is given credit for the development of the close-up, the fades, and parallel action. Close-ups and fades are described in the material on photography on pages 129–137. Parallel action means the development of two or more stories which are united near the end. In other words, there will be two stories both of which are intensely interesting, and the picture will cut alternately from one story to the other, perhaps leaving the heroine of one theme in a dangerous position while the other story continues. This was done, for example, in "The Birth of a Nation."

What are the unusual qualities found in Griffith's work? Paul Rotha points out that Griffith developed his story

> . . . so as to intensify the final struggle of the theme by using the conflicting elements of nature, of rain, snow, storm, and ice. This use of atmospheric environment heightened the Griffith climax to an almost indescribable pitch of emotion, well seen in the snowstorm, and melting river of ice and the awe-inspiring waterfall of "Way Down East." It will be remembered that the elements increased in intensity towards the final struggle. In this example from "Way Down East," Griffith used not only the available natural resources, but heightened the thrill of the rescue from the waterfall by the capabilities of the camera itself by contrasting two streams of movement. In this sequence of events, the snowstorm, the ice-floes, and the waterfall, each increasing in strength, formed a comparative background to the increasing despair of the characters themselves in the narrative. . . .

> The "last-minute-rescue," such a prominent feature of the Griffith film, had been used at an early date in "The Life of an American Fireman" (1903), and has been in constant employment since then. The girl at the guillotine; the knife about to fall; the approaching riders flourishing the pardon; the little details that hinder the fall of the knife; the arrival of the riders

THE KID   *First National*

Charlie Chaplin, actor and director. Compare Jackie Coogan in this picture with the illustration on page 225, which shows him in the rôle of Tom Sawyer.

at the last moment; these are the factors, so well used in "Orphans of the Storm," familiar to all audiences throughout the world. Griffith improved the tension created by parallel action by addition of the close-up. He interspaced the alternative motives with a close-up of the hooves of galloping horses; the keen edge of the blade; the girl's neck bared; the excitement on the faces of the crowd; tears in the eyes of Miss Gish—and so on.[1]

No pictures by D. W. Griffith have been available to viewers in this country for the past year. One picture produced by him in 1931 titled "The Struggle," was a failure and was shown in only a few theaters. If you ever have an opportunity to attend a picture directed by Griffith, however, go there and learn what you can. You will have the opportunity, then, to see a picture directed by a man who will doubtless go down in motion-picture history as one of the greatest of the early directors.

Another remarkable director is Charles Chaplin. Yes, this is the same Charlie Chaplin whose antics delight you on the screen. Perhaps you did not realize that he writes and directs his own pictures. The unique part of Chaplin's work is his avoidance of dialogue in his films. He must, therefore, express meaning in greater degree through gesture and titles. In his last film, "City Lights," he used sound but not speech. To quote again from Paul Rotha:

> Like other great directors, Chaplin makes supreme use of camera emphasis. Little movements mean big things in the Chaplin film, and, moreover, his invention of detail is amazing. Three memorable instances occur to the mind. The unforgettable roll dance in "The Gold Rush;" the inimitable crooked finger, suggestive of the maggot in the apple, in "The Circus;" and the magnificent pantomime scene of the David and Goliath sermon in "The Pilgrim." [2]

[1] Rotha, Paul, *The Film Till Now*, pp. 88–89.
[2] *Op. cit.*, p. 101.

The name of Ernst Lubitsch is one with which you ought to be familiar. Among his earlier pictures are, "The Student Prince," "The Patriot," "Du Barry," "The Flame," "Anne Boleyn," and among later pictures are, "The Smiling Lieutenant," "The Love Parade," and "One Hour with You." "The Patriot" was extremely well done; but Lubitsch had a great advantage in this picture; he was directing an exceedingly able actor, Emil Jannings.

In *Time*, the following biographical comment concerning Lubitsch appeared:

Son of a Berlin shopkeeper, Ernst Lubitsch was made to work in his father's store while he learned enough about acting to get a job with Max Reinhardt. In 1913 he performed in cinema for the first time, liked it so much he never went back to the stage. He went to Hollywood to direct Mary Pickford in "Rosita" nine years ago, after making himself and Pola Negri famous with "Gypsy Blood," "Montmarte," "One Arabian Night," and "Du Barry" (called "Passion" in the United States).

Short, swarthy, scowling, Director Lubitsch has a Teutonic sense of humor, a juvenile liking for jokes. . . . More Teutonic than his humor is the Lubitsch urge for order and completion. Before making a picture he spends three months preparing the script with his writers, telling them exactly what he wants. When the script—essentially a stenographic record of a Lubitsch idea—is finished, he seldom sees it for he knows it all by heart. In staff conferences he is charmed to argue over details, pleased when a costumer asks advice about a button on the hero's coat. . . .

When someone tells him he has made a clumsy sequence, Lubitsch says: "I wanted it that way," trumps up a complicated reason. He says: "I discard rules in making pictures. . . . Whatever fits best, I use."

Actors who might resent his arrogance in any less intelligent director, are pleased by his appreciation. Saturated in the cinema, Lubitsch diverts himself when not making real pictures by making a cast out of his friends, his servants, the people who pass him on the street. "Ach," he says, "you are a crook. No, you are head of a gang of blackmailers . . . you know everything, everybody." Pleased in his prowess in such conceits, he assumes a wise expression and rolls his eyes—the cameras for an endless hypothetical scenario.[1]

King Vidor is, without doubt, one of the best directors in Hollywood today. His picture "The Crowd," which is a story of the common man and his progress in the city, was splendidly done. It shows how human personalities are submerged and crushed by our huge cities. Comments have been made elsewhere on the motion picture "Hallelujah," another of King Vidor's pictures, which probably is one of his best works. You may be interested in knowing that the leading character in this play, Daniel Haynes, later acted the part of Adam in "Green Pastures," a play which ran in New York for more than a year and then toured the country. "The Big Parade" was also done by King Vidor and was a popular success.

The motion picture "Street Scene," which King Vidor directed, was one of the finest pictures of the year in which it appeared. In this film he had the problem of making a motion picture which did not shift its location from the beginning to the end. Heywood Broun declared that the motion picture was better than the stage play.

The ability of Josef von Sternberg is impressive, but as yet he has not directed a picture of fundamental value. Some critics, however, give him a great deal of credit for his picture "The Salvation Hunters," released a number of years ago. Among his later films, are, "The Last Command," "The Docks of New York," "Monte Carlo," "Thunderbolt," "Paying the Penalty," "Dishonored," "Morocco," and "Shanghai Express." His pictures show a great deal of

[1] February 1, 1932.

technical expertness, but the last few films which he has directed have been so trivial in theme that their chief merits lay in the skillful technical direction given them. If Von Sternberg is given stories which have some fundamental meaning in them, he may produce some truly valuable motion pictures.

An interesting type of picture is one for which Robert Flaherty is responsible, namely, "Nanook of the North," and "Moana." They may be described in part as documentary films, since the strength of the picture lies not in the story but in the authentic backgrounds presented. Did you like the picture "Grass," "Chang," and "Rango"? Ernest B. Schoedsack and Merian C. Cooper directed them.

A director who does whimsical and fantastic things well is Herbert Brenon. Some of his well-known pictures are, "The Daughter of the Gods," "Peter Pan," "A Kiss for Cinderella," "The Side-Show of Life," "The Alaskan," "The Little French Girl," "Beau Geste," "Sorrell and Son," and "The Case of Sergeant Grischa."

Another able director is Frank Borzage. "Street Angel," "Seventh Heaven," and "A Farewell to Arms," are among his pictures. In 1932 he won the award of the Academy of Motion Picture Arts and Sciences for his direction of the picture "Bad Girl."

Where Do the Directors Come from?

Where do these directors come from? What influences have led them to this type of work? Are there certain "schools" of directing (and here I use the word not as an educational institution, but rather as a term to describe a group of persons who are using similar methods)? No, the profession of motion-picture directing is not old enough for that.

THUNDER OVER MEXICO   *Principal Pictures*

Sergei Eisenstein's genius in selecting native actors and in developing scenes of great pictorial beauty is here illustrated.

When we look up the history of noted directors, as we can in the *Film Daily Directors' Annual and Production Guide*, we see that Frank Borzage, Cecil B. De Mille, Wesley Ruggles, and Herbert Brenon have had extensive experience in acting. Frank Capra, King Vidor, and Lewis Milestone have been associated with the industry in a variety of fields, two of them beginning as prop boy and advancing through various stages, such as assistant cameraman, cameraman, art director, and so on. It is likely that a careful study of the work of each of these directors would show traces of that early training.

What about the future? Will there be a shift in the training that directors will have had? Undoubtedly. We may expect that a literature will grow up dealing with direction. Certainly a director ought to have had a good deal of preliminary training in working with lighting and photography. He should have had some training in dramatic art. That does not mean that he should be skillful enough actually to play in motion pictures, yet he ought to have had enough contact with acting to have a feeling for it.

FOREIGN DIRECTORS

If you have an ambition to gain intelligent knowledge of the direction of motion pictures, you should know some of the work of Eisenstein and Pudovkin, directors of Russian pictures. About two years ago Eisenstein came to this country to direct motion pictures for one of the large producers, but unfortunately no pictures were made. Eisenstein then went to Mexico and directed a picture which was released under the title "Thunder over Mexico." You ought to see it because it represents an approach to motion-picture making which is widely different from that commonly seen in Hollywood productions.

The Russians, of course, have thought of the film as a device by means of which they can acquaint every Russian with the aims of their five-year program and the alleged superiority of the Soviet way of life. Their films, therefore, are frankly propaganda and seek to express in a vivid fashion just what the Soviet government is doing. A number of these films—"October," "Storm over Asia," "Potemkin," and others—have been shown in this country. If you have an opportunity to see such pictures, you should do so, especially if you are interested in the technical and social possibilities of the cinema.

Another foreign director is René Clair, a Frenchman. His latest film, "A Nous la Liberté," has been shown in the larger cities of this country. Mordaunt Hall, film critic of the *New York Times*, called it one of the ten best pictures of 1932. Clair makes only one film each year, and this is truly his own. He writes his own scenarios, directs his own pictures, cuts and edits his own film. In spite of the difficulty of seeing pictures directed by René Clair, we are including this short discussion in order to acquaint high-school and college students with the name of an exceedingly capable motion-picture director.

The Director and the Writer

We can expect that the director and writer of the story each has a peculiar and unique contribution to make to the spectators who view that story on the screen. If the contribution of the writer or the director shows no discernment or genius in the portrayal of character, or if there is nothing unique in the method of telling the story, then we can hardly characterize these men as able. Or if they continue to tell their stories in the same fashion in which they have always told them, we may also doubt their artistic ability. True artistry does not repeat itself.

As I have pointed out, many directors have combined authorship with their directing activities, and there is a rather widespread feeling that this combination is desirable. Here is what Robert Sherwood, well-known playwright and critic, has to say about it in the December, 1931, issue of the *Hollywood Spectator:*

> Some time ago, Dalton Trumbo said in the SPECTATOR that the director of a picture and the author of its story should be one and the same person. With that theory I am in the most complete agreement.
>
> It has always applied to the stage, and I am firmly of the belief that it also applies to the screen. Like any other good rule it leaves openings for exceptions, of course; but I can't imagine any valid argument against the doctrine that the man who conceives an idea is, in most cases, best qualified to give it expression. (I am referring only to full-blown ideas, not to those which are mere haphazard suggestions for others to carry out.)
>
> Shakespeare staged his own plays. So did Molière and Sheridan. So does Shaw. So do Marc Connelly, George Kaufman, Winchell Smith, Noel Coward, Elmer Rice, George Kelly, Owen Davis and (often) Sidney Howard and Philip Barry. I confess that I don't, being one of those introverted unfortunates who can't give directions to others (except in print); but I'd be much better off if I could.
>
> The greatest motion pictures that have ever been made were written and directed by one man. He even went so far as to act in them all, save one, "A Woman of Paris." [Mr. Sherwood is referring to Charles Chaplin.]
>
> It may be argued that most authors know nothing about the technic of motion picture direction, and that most directors know nothing about the development of a dramatic theme.
>
> The answer is—in both cases—that they should.
>
> It has ever been the practice of the movie people to rely on collaborative effort: one or more men to furnish the plot, another

group to prepare a treatment, more to arrange the continuity, many more to fill in the dialogue and then, ultimately, some supreme being to direct the completed mess. Now and then that process has produced admirable results, but only by accident.

There has been nothing accidental in the quality of the long, magnificent procession of Chaplin comedies. They are the works of one man who combines creative intelligence with a superb mastery of the medium of his expression.

The same may be said of the works of William Shakespeare, Ludwig von Beethoven, Leonardo da Vinci, Phidias, or any other artist that you care to name (provided you are the type that cares to name artists).

That this viewpoint is shared by others is demonstrated by the following quotations from the *Film Daily Directors' Annual and Production Guide*. *The Film Daily* sent a questionnaire to a number of the leading motion-picture critics of the country, and here are two critics' statements concerning the director. W. Ward Marsh, of the Cleveland *Plain Dealer*, says:

> The director should be in on the story from its very inception, either writing it or else collaborating with the author. The director's work does not end when he puts his microphone aside. It should go on until the film has been cut and edited and ready for market. If he is a good director, he knows exactly what he wants. Turning photographed celluloid over to the cutters and editors permits a new force to enter and they may entirely change, often ruin, the very thing the director has worked so hard to put into his picture. A good director is the very life's blood of a picture, and he can turn a banal story into something vitally interesting. A poor director can wreck the best script.

Substantially the same point of view is presented by Thornton Delahanty, of the New York *Evening Post:*

> The director is potentially the most important factor in picture production. A bungling, inept director can ruin a good

story idea and he can make hams out of most good actors. He can confuse the plot with too much detail, or by failing to point it properly. Lacking visual imagination or a sense of tempo, a director is almost certain to destroy that vitality and inventiveness which are necessary to good entertainment. Naturally, the converse of this is true. A resourceful director can take mediocre players and stories and make them seem fresh and original. Under an ideal state, the director should be encouraged to write his own stories. Then he will visualize them in terms of the motion picture, and the result will be a picture that really moves.. When you have directors instead of writers creating stories you will have less dialogue and more action, and it is a matter of record that the most successful talkies are those in which the appeal is to the eye rather than to the ear.

Finally, Mrs. Frances Taylor Patterson, in her book titled *Scenario and Screen*, paints this picture of the "ideal" director:

> Of course the ideal director should combine the actor, the artist, the painter, the sculptor, the dramatist, and the technical camera expert in one. The amalgam of all these, plus perhaps a bit of the architect, of the psychologist, and of the critic, would be in very truth the perfect director.[1]

WHAT IS GOOD DIRECTING?

Now that you have been introduced to some able motion-picture directors, let us think about the qualities of good motion-picture directing. How can you tell whether a picture has been well directed or not? Perhaps the best way of illustrating this would be to have a series of shots taken of identical situations using the same characters but with different directors; then you could see just what variations exist. It will be impossible to carry out this plan until we have films which can be used to illustrate such books as

[1] Patterson, Frances Taylor, *Scenario and Screen*, p. 125.

this, and I think that we shall not have to wait long for them. Until that time, however, we must do the best we can with descriptions of good and poor motion-picture direction.

THE GOOD DIRECTOR

The first important quality of a good director is that he must know a good story when he sees it. In other words, he ought to be able to take the synopsis (outline) of a story and visualize the motion picture that could be made from that story. Many short stories and novels do not make good motion pictures, for there are not enough visual elements in them. Pictures are not abstract; they are concrete. You cannot make a picture of the word "love." You can, however, show people in love and express the meaning of the word in this fashion. Unless a director is able to take the synopsis and develop the picture in his imagination to see how effective it will be, he is not going to get the most out of his medium.

Some motion pictures are made and then tossed into the junk heap either before they have been shown to the public or shortly after because they are "flops." This is because some director, or at least the person responsible for the making of that picture, thought there was a motion picture in it when there really was not. An able director, then knows a good story when he sees it, and must be able to distinguish between plots which are suitable, let us say, for a stage drama, for a novel, for a short story, or a motion-picture presentation.

Second, a good director must have an interest in the picture he is making. Everyone knows that one does best in those things in which he has a personal interest. Is it not good reasoning to expect that a director will be more likely to succeed with those stories in which he has a personal con-

cern? I venture to forecast that in the future we shall have
more pictures made by directors who are working on stories
which they really want to put into films. When a director
is asked to make a film for which he has no sympathy, one
which does not enlist his enthusiasm, the product is likely
to be unsatisfactory. Of course, the public may not always
enjoy and support a picture which the director thinks is
exceedingly good. In spite of this difficulty, however, we
should probably not have more "flops" under the new system, and we might have more successes.

The successes will come because of an interesting fact.
A director who must make the pictures that are assigned
to him, whether he wants to do them or not, may become a
mere mechanic; that is, he may make motion pictures in
a routine fashion, not adding that extra bit of genius and
creativeness which distinguishes the artist from the artisan.
This point is well illustrated by a story which Tolstoy tells
about the Russian artist Bruloff. Once when correcting a
pupil's study, Bruloff just touched it in a few places, and the
poor study immediately became worth while. "Why, you
only touched it a wee bit, and it is quite another thing!"
said one of the pupils. "Art begins where the wee bit begins,"
replied Bruloff.

*Third, a good director must know what the camera can
do, what it cannot do, what it ought to do, and what it
ought not to do.* Because a camera can do certain things,
some directors think that it must; and, consequently, the
screen is marred by all sorts of outlandish, freakish shots
which have no connection with the picture. They are there
merely because the director wants to show off the stunts
the camera is capable of performing.

Fourth, a good director must know the art of story-telling.
A good story-teller always knows what his climax is, and

makes every part contribute to it. The director also has the responsibility of always keeping his story moving forward in the swiftest possible way. Sometimes, of course, he must stop the action or slow it down in order to develop characterizations properly. If he does not do this, the story may not be clear, and the characterizations will be confused. But he must do no more than this, for when he uses scenes that are not really helpful in achieving the climax, he has slowed down the forward movement of the story and to some degree has marred it.

Fifth, the good director not only must have the story well in mind and know exactly what he is trying to picture on the screen, but he must also be able to convey his ideas to the players and inspire them with a desire to interpret the meaning properly. Did you ever see a motion picture and have the feeling that the actors did not quite know what it was all about? The reason for their apparent confusion was probably the fact that they really did not understand the relation of their parts to the whole plot or to the director's complete plan. They had merely gone through their actions as puppets under the control of the director, and their wooden acting showed clearly their ignorance of what the play meant. A good director will talk over all action in advance with his actors; he will discuss each scene in detail with them; he will help each actor to make his rôle stand out sharply. Of course, he will not be able to tell the actor exactly how things are to be done; the actor must be able to contribute that much, since that is his share, and the part about which he should know more than anyone else. However, it seems that the director might well make known to the actor just what is wanted; if the director can do that, he has done enough.

Sixth, a good director must know how to edit a picture in order to achieve the proper effects. Of course, if he has followed the other requirements of story-telling he has much less of a task, but it is impossible to construct a motion picture that is absolutely perfect as it is filmed. It may be necessary to cut out a scene in one part and perhaps to add something in another, to change the music that has been used for certain scenes, or to shorten a scene that is too long. The proof of the director's ability lies in putting the picture together so that the story is told in the most effective way. If he can do that, he deserves the honor of being called a creative director.

"DIRECTORIAL TOUCHES"

One way in which this creativeness shows itself is in what are called "directorial touches." Here are some examples: In "Sweepings," Eric Linden has just been told by his father (Lionel Barrymore) to get out of the house. Linden goes out the front door jauntily; the camera then tilts down to a view of his legs as he trips down the steps. His shoes and trousers are new and well kept. Next we see another shot of legs, but the shoes are not shined and the trousers are not pressed. The third shot of the legs, still walking along, shows a more halting step, poorer shoes, poorer trousers. And finally the legs stop at a table in a cheap hotel or rooming house and the camera then for the first time pans (see glossary for definition) up to give us a view of the young man, who has now been reduced to poverty.

In the motion picture "Cimarron," George Stone, playing the part of a Jew, is brutally handled by a ruffian and is thrown to the ground. It seemed as if the crude sticks which were back of his upraised hands as he fell were thrown together roughly in the form of a cross, thus bringing to the audience another symbol of the persecution of the Jews.

Conclusion

Why do not the directors turn out better pictures? Is it because they don't care? One person closely connected with the industry says that they do care: "There is not a director in the business who does not hope to have his name go down in motion-picture history as the creator of some great motion picture, but most of them are given a script two weeks before production starts, and are expected to make a box-office picture in 18 or 21 days. It is the producer, and not the director, who is to blame for this."

QUESTIONS FOR REVIEW

Here are some questions that members of the class may wish to ask themselves after they have seen a photoplay. Perhaps those in your group can find other questions which they wish to add, or they may wish to change this list.

1. Did the actors and actresses seem to understand what the play was about?
2. Do you believe the director was able to handle all types of scenes well—comedy, tragedy, farce?
3. Did the picture give evidence of being well edited? If not, what scenes would you have eliminated?
4. Where were scenes needed that were not included?
5. Give some examples of "directorial touches" that were used.
6. What especially noteworthy examples did you see of the use of moving shots? Close-ups? Angle shots?

CHAPTER XII

WHAT ARE MOTION PICTURES FOR?

IN the last few pages standards for acting, direction, photography, and lighting, have been discussed. But a motion picture is more than a collection of these individual items. Each of these parts must be combined with the others in such a way as to make a *good* motion picture, a picture which has a unity of its own.

Perhaps you have never asked yourself this question: What are motion pictures for? It is an important one nevertheless. The question of *purpose* is one that thinking people must ask, not only about motion pictures, but also about schools, churches, industry, about life itself. What, then, are motion pictures for?

I once asked a group of high-school students this question, and these are a few of the answers which I received:

"They give the audience some fun and entertainment."
"They keep me from getting bored with life."
"They give people pleasure."
"They make you forget your troubles."
"It's somewhere to go when you have a date."
"It's a place to go at night."
"It's just a way to kill time."
"It's a way to learn about life."
"You learn what happens when you make certain choices."
"They show what people do under different circumstances."
"It gives you the artist's idea of life."

The idea of the motion picture expressed by the first seven of these high-school students is the one usually held.

Many people think the motion picture is like a drug—something that takes them away from the pain of the harsh, cruel world in which they live and brings them into a world of delightful make-believe and fancy. At the end of two hours, they go back into the world, sometimes better able to face its problems, sometimes more discouraged than ever.

These persons believe that the purpose of the motion picture is to make you forget, not remember; to make you dream, not think; to get you farther away from the world in which you live, not closer to it; to flatter you, never to make you see yourself as you really are; to remove you from the important happenings of everyday life into the movie world of unimportant events. Iris Barry in her book, *Let's Go to the Movies*, phrases the purpose of the motion picture in this way: "It is not intended to edify, it is not designed to instruct, or move, or thrill. It is primarily a something to banish care, even reflection, even consciousness. The cinema is a drug." [1]

The last four answers express a purpose which the motion picture might carry out. I believe that the students who wrote these last four answers have a much clearer picture of what the motion picture might do than do the first seven. It is my own belief that the motion picture is an art as important as music, literature, painting, or the drama, and that a conception of the motion picture merely as idle entertainment for idle people is too limited.

Through the motion picture we can have displayed for us the finest responses that our finest individuals have been able to make in certain important decisions of life. In other words, it can provide patterns for the highest and most intelligent conduct of which man is capable. It can show us characters trying to discover what is most valuable in life

[1] Page 53.

and the methods which they use to achieve their goals. Of course, different characters will have different ideas about what is valuable, but the spectator will be able to view these different types of conduct and see which one fits in best with the kind of life which he wants to live.

When an individual distinguishes himself by a particular type of conduct, we ought to be able to point to some motion picture and say, "An example of such conduct was presented there." Through the vision of the artist, whether it be in music, in literature, in painting, in statuary, in dramatics, we catch an understanding of the most valuable and finest experiences that the race has ever known. It should be so with motion pictures also. The motion picture, therefore, is too fine an instrument to be used only for passing entertainment or to kill time.

THE MOVIES CAN HELP US THINK THROUGH OUR PROBLEMS

The motion picture, then, can give us data about life. For example, if you carry out an experiment in chemistry or physics or general science, you find that when you ignite illuminating gas and air mixed in a certain proportion, you get a loud explosion. If you always mix them in the same proportion, you always get this explosion. In the same way the motion picture can give us this data as to what happens when people make certain choices. The criminal breaks the law; he is arrested. Another criminal breaks a law; he may not be arrested. However, though he may escape legal punishment he is cut off from friendly relationships with many of his acquaintances. Harmful consequences occur to his family because of his conduct. The motion picture should teach us that in life certain effects follow from certain causes.

H. G. Wells has spoken about the purpose of the novel. If you will substitute the words "motion picture" for "novel" you will get a clear notion as to what the motion picture might do. This quotation is important enough to be read aloud and discussed in detail in class. Is this really the purpose of the motion picture?

You see now the scope of the claim I am making for the novel: it is to be the social mediator, the vehicle of understanding, the instrument of self-examination, the parade of morals and the exchange of manners, the factory of customs and ideas, the criticism of laws and institutions and of social dogmas and ideas. It is to be the home confessional, the initiator of knowledge, the seed of fruitful self-questioning. Let me be very clear here, I do not mean for a moment that the novelist is going to set up as a teacher, as a sort of priest, with a pen, who will make men and women believe and do this and that. The novel is not a new sort of pulpit. . . . But the novelist is going to present conduct, devise beautiful conduct, discuss conduct, analyze conduct, suggest conduct, illuminate it through and through. . . .

We are going to write, subject only to our own limitations, about the whole of human life. We are going to deal with political questions and religious questions and social questions. We cannot present people unless we have this free hand, this unrestricted field. . . .

We are going to write about it all . . . until a thousand pretences and ten thousand impostures shrivel in the cold, clear air of our elucidations. We are going to write of wasted opportunities and latent beauties, until a thousand new ways of living open to men and women.[1]

The motion picture, then, should show you just what problems people are facing today and the different ways that these problems can be solved. They should show you the consequences of certain ways of solving problems so that you may know what to expect if you try to work out your problems as did the persons on the screen. This means,

[1] Wells, H. G., "The Contemporary Novel," *Atlantic Monthly*, Vol. CIX (January, 1912), pp. 6, 10, 11.

PETER PAN

This picture illustrates the value of the motion picture in portraying fantasy.

of course, that you must carefully study the solutions that are given to important life problems, because they may not be sound ones. Indeed, that is the chief source of danger to children and youths in viewing motion pictures. Many solutions given in the motion pictures are unsound and therefore dangerous to those who have not thought through the problems. The solution of the race question shown in "The Birth of a Nation" certainly was unsatisfactory to many thinking persons.

For example, what should you do when you have an opportunity to obtain political advancement at the expense of your ideals? Yancey Cravat in "Cimarron" decided that it was far better to give up the governorship of the state than to surrender his ideals concerning the Indians. In "Arrowsmith" the hero, played by Ronald Coleman, must make this decision: whether to carry out his scientific experiment and, if necessary, let people die; or to give up this experiment and to save people's lives. He chose the latter policy. In "Emma" the heroine, played by Marie Dressler, decided that service to children in a family was more important to her than wealth. In "Oliver Twist" Nancy aids Oliver even though it means that she loses her own life because of it.

Perhaps this is too serious a way of looking at the motion picture. Not everyone will agree with the statement of the purpose of the motion picture that we have just made. One editorial writer asks why some persons object to the frivolity and shallowness of our motion pictures. He says that their purpose is to entertain, and, if they must distort beauty and sweeten the bitter to do this, they are only presenting life in the artificial form that is most fascinating to the ordinary person. The purpose of motion pictures, he says, is not to make people more intelligent about the world in which they live. Motion pictures do not have, he maintains, and should

not have, any social message. He says they frankly appeal
to the senses and have no purpose except to lift the members
of the audience out of their drab and meaningless lives for
an hour or two. According to him, life is certainly serious enough without seeing more of it when we go to the
movies.

Is there some truth in this statement? Is it in complete
opposition to the opinion adapted from H. G. Wells? Do
you think that there would be danger if this view were taken
as the only purpose of motion pictures?

SOCIAL VALUES IN MOTION PICTURES

There is one serious danger in the idea that the purpose of motion pictures is only to entertain. They do more
than entertain, whether we wish it or not. Scientists who
have studied the effect of motion pictures on children and
youth have discovered that boys and girls and young men
and women remember a great deal of what they see at the
movies. And, unlike some lessons they get out of books, there
is little forgetting.

We know, too, that young people who saw the picture
"The Birth of a Nation" were influenced unfavorably toward
Negroes by seeing it. "Welcome Danger" influenced them
against the Chinese. "Four Sons" made them like the
Germans more. "All Quiet on the Western Front" gave
them a more unfavorable attitude toward war. The boys
and girls who went to see these motion pictures may have
wanted only to be entertained, nevertheless their information, attitudes, and conduct were changed by that experience.

"But," you may say, "is it really true that inaccurate and
harmful ideas are shown in motion pictures? Aren't the goals
that the leading characters are trying to reach important and

worth-while ones?" In order to show that there are many commonplace and even harmful goals in motion pictures, I want to give you these facts. Here are the goals that the leading characters in 115 motion pictures were trying to reach. Out of 883 goals, 63 per cent were individual goals; 28 per cent, personal; and 9 per cent, social. By individual goals I mean ones where the character is trying to get something for himself. For example, a man may try to win the love of a girl, or he may be interested primarily in financial success. A personal goal involves the happiness, not only of the person himself but of some one else near or dear to him. An example of a personal goal is the protection of a loved one or an attempt to avenge another person. A social goal involves a much larger group of persons, and includes such goals as philanthropy and scientific achievement.

The most frequent of all the goals sought for was an individual goal, namely, "winning another's love." This goal was found in 70 per cent of the pictures. Certainly, this is a worth-while goal, but many people would believe that this much emphasis upon it is undesirable. The second most frequent individual goal was "marriage for love," and this appeared in 36 per cent of the pictures. The kind of love we are talking about here is romantic love, not love for parents or friends. Interestingly enough, in the personal goals, those dealing with love are also emphasized. "Happiness of a loved one" is found as a goal in 27 per cent of the pictures, "protection of a loved one" in 15 per cent, and "rescue of a loved one" in 12 per cent.

Perhaps you are not convinced that all this emphasis on love really has a harmful effect. Perhaps you really do not believe that there are other important goals that have been crowded out because of this emphasis on love. I would suggest that you discuss in class the goals of the leading characters in the books that you are reading in your English classes. What are the goals of the leading characters in such books as *Treasure Island, Ivanhoe, A Tale of Two Cities, A Christmas Carol, Ben-Hur, The Story of the Other Wise Man,* Helen Keller's *Story of My Life, The Man without a Country, Little Women,* Franklin's *Autobiography, Silas Marner, David Copperfield, Sohrab and Rustum, The King of the Golden River, Dr. Jekyll and Mr. Hyde.*

Social goals were the least common of the three kinds—individual, personal, and social. Social goals appeared in 20 per cent of the pictures. Most of them, however, involved the performance of duty by a policeman, a soldier, or some other public officer. Only rarely do we see in the motion pictures men who have in mind not individual, not personal goals, but goals that covered all of humanity. We need to see pictured more often the goals that are sought by such characters as Helen Keller, Jane Addams, Sir Wilfred Grenfell, Julius Rosenwald, Gandhi, and others.

An Unbalanced Diet

Another practice which is probably not to the credit of the movies is their emphasis on and treatment of sex and of crime. In 1930, 27 per cent of the motion pictures produced were classifiable as crime, and 15 per cent as sex pictures. That is, crime and sex accounted for 42 per cent of the motion pictures in 1930. Does this overemphasize crime and sex? Again, I would ask you to think of your library or the books which are on recommended lists. I doubt very much whether you will find anything like this proportion of books on these subjects. Some of them, however, deal with these problems. Do you think the treatment of sex and of crime in the movies is as artistic and thoughtful as it is in the best of literature? Is it in good taste? Or is it cheap and inartistic?

In the next picture you see which deals with crime, ask yourself these questions:

1. Did it give some insight as to the fundamental causes of criminal behavior?
2. Did it show the strong and weak points of our present methods of legal justice?
3. Did it leave the impression that punishing the criminal solves the problem of crime?
4. Did it show the great inadequacies of our modern methods of handling criminals in our jails and penitentiaries?

It may be illuminating for you to ask your social-studies teacher to comment on causes and cures for crime. President Hoover appointed a commission to study this problem, and its report is contained in a volume titled *Report on the Causes of Crime, National Commission on Law Observance and Enforcement.* If you have an opportunity to read this book, ask yourself this question: Do the motion pictures treat crime honestly and accurately?

I think we are also safe in saying that motion-picture treatment of crime is too simple. It leads you to believe that we shall solve the problem of crime merely by having our laws better enforced, or by passing new laws. You have probably learned in your social-studies courses that we shall not get anywhere in solving the crime problem until we really understand the causes of crime. Once in a while there is a motion picture which helps us understand this problem. "Young America," in which Spencer Tracy, Doris Kenyon, and Ralph Bellamy appeared, showed how juvenile-court officers used intelligence in preventing youth from leading lives of crime. "I Am a Fugitive from a Chain Gang" gave us much information about legal injustices, but did not show us just what causes lie back of the chain gang itself. By the way, what are those causes?

Overemphasis on Luxury

Another criticism that can be made of the movies is that they overemphasize luxurious standards of living. For example, in the study of motion pictures it was discovered that 22 per cent of the residences shown in 115 pictures were extremely wealthy, 49 per cent were wealthy, 24 per cent moderate, 4 per cent were definitely poor, and 1 per cent could not be classified easily. You see, when we combine the extremely wealthy and the wealthy groups, we get 71 per cent of all the residences. In other words, there were almost three times as many wealthy and extremely wealthy residences shown as moderate residences.

Is it a good thing for an audience habitually to see luxury on the screen since most of them do not have it at home? Perhaps it gives them happy daydreams of a kind of life that is denied to them, but which they may enjoy viewing. What do you think about it?

Unreality in Motion Pictures

In most cases, the harm that comes is caused by the untruthfulness or inaccuracy in the picture. In one picture, for example, a gambler who was also a murderer is killed at the end of the picture. Some persons who saw this picture, however, must have felt that he had lived an adventuresome life, and they may have desired to follow his footsteps. Indeed, he was shown as powerful, well-dressed, attractive, and admired by many. His sudden death by a rival gangster's bullet might not be enough to keep certain persons from imitating the life that he led. Some who saw the picture might even think that they could be smart enough to avoid that bullet, live to a ripe old age, and enjoy all the profits of their gambling activities. Do you think there is any danger in showing gangsters and criminals as more attractive than they really are, even though they are killed or put in prison at the end of the picture? As one high-school youth put it: "I enjoy a Cagney film; I like Jimmy tremendously; but he is too likeable a little chap to make the way of life he portrays seem disagreeable and un-wise."

In another motion picture, a young man and woman decide to live luxuriously as long as they can on money which the young man has stolen. When it is spent, they plan to commit suicide together. In the end, however, the young man gives himself up to the police. The impression is left with the audience that a wealthy man who has befriended the girl will use his influence to get the young man a speedy release from prison. Unfortunately, throughout the story the two criminals are shown as appealing and romantic youngsters. The picture thus drawn may prove harmful because of its inaccuracy. Persons who would do this sort of thing are not likely to be the delightful, charming, kindly pair we see in the picture. That it might possibly happen is not the question. That it is a likely occurrence, however, is clearly to be doubted. Further, the effects of an act of this kind are not lightly erased even by a prison sentence. The picture leads us to believe that after serving a prison term, probably short, the two lovers will be reunited to live happily ever after. This is not going to be an easy task, is it? Will not society, with good reason, distrust and shun them? And nowhere in the film is this shown. Did this picture hurt the children and youth who saw it? It is hard to know, but these are problems which are important for class discussion.

THE NEED FOR BALANCE

Perhaps we should not try to discover the single purpose of motion pictures. Perhaps there are many purposes—purposes as varied as life itself. Possibly the significant fact about motion pictures is that, like life, they should be proportioned properly—not all seriousness, not all frivolity. A proper balance should be sought.

Some motion pictures provide that diversification or balance within themselves. They, like life, combine tragedy with comedy, lightness with seriousness. Sometimes this is done successfully, sometimes unsuccessfully. Other motion pictures hold consistently to a single theme. If something light and frivolous is being presented, the spirit is kept throughout the picture; if the picture is one that has a serious or tragic theme, a serious tone is maintained.

But no matter which method is used in the pictures you see, you should study them. Are your motion pictures giving you a well-balanced diet, or are you getting too much sugar and whipped cream? If you are unthinkingly attending every light, frothy comedy that comes to your theater, then your motion-picture diet is decidedly unbalanced. On the other hand, this may be said just as truthfully of a diet which consists almost exclusively of tragedies, hair-raising mystery stories, wild western tales, or the smart, sophisticated "drawing-room dramas." Even though a film is well diversified, it still tends to fall more or less distinctly into a class, and care should be used in one's selection of pictures.

QUESTIONS FOR REVIEW

Here are some questions that you might have in mind when you think about the motion pictures that you have seen.

1. What are the chief goals sought by the leading attractive characters? Are they selfish or unselfish goals? Do they closely resemble goals you and your friends are trying to reach? Are they better or worse?
2. How is crime treated in the picture? Does the picture present the criminal ready made, or does it show you the conditions of his life which caused him to turn to crime? Are the consequences of crime truthfully shown? Are crime and criminals shown in such a way as to invite imitation?
3. Does the motion picture emphasize the idea that romantic love or happy marriages are largely an accident, or does it show them as resulting from thoughtful planning and hard work? Which way do you think they ought to be shown?
4. What inconsistencies did you notice in the actions of the characters?
5. Are physical beauty and luxury overemphasized?
6. Is violence, either in terms of fighting or war, shown as a desirable method of settling disputes?
7. What is the attitude taken toward Negroes, Mexicans, Chinese, and other underprivileged groups?
8. Do you approve of the ideals of home life shown in the picture?
9. Is anything shown that was cheap or in poor taste?
10. Do the motion pictures give you much insight into industrial, commercial, or agricultural activities?
11. What is the total impression given you by the picture of the nature of American life and people? Of foreign life and people?
12. Does this picture give any help in solving your everyday problems? Should it?

CHAPTER XIII

WHAT NEXT?

THE chief aim throughout this entire book has been to increase your enjoyment of motion pictures. We have tried to do that by pointing out new and different things to look for at the motion pictures, values that otherwise might have remained hidden. This discovery and comparison of values is something you do not only at the motion-picture theater, but you are doing it every waking hour of your life. For example, you must choose between different foods at a cafeteria, the kind of suit or dress that you will buy, the college that you plan to attend, or the work you will follow.

In all these choices your measuring sticks are certain standards. As you read this manual you should have developed a series of standards for judging motion pictures. That set of standards, however, is not complete. You must continually experiment with them, revising whenever necessary. They are, therefore, tentative standards.

It is no longer necessary to attend the first motion picture you happen upon, blindly taking a chance on its merits, any more than an intelligent shopper need buy the first article inspected, regardless of quality and appropriateness. You have learned to select, using your standards as a basis for this selection. Of course, you have made mistakes and you will continue to make them, but such mistakes will be fewer as time goes on. And you will, I am sure, be disappointed less often in pictures for which you have "shopped" than you would be under the hit-and-miss system of attending whatever picture happened to be shown at the nearest theater.

Although we have tried to make this manual as interesting and as practical as possible, there are, of course, many ideas which would have added to its value, but which are not yet practical. For example, words are not entirely satisfactory for bringing out certain facts about motion pictures. We shall soon be able to present some of this material as lectures or discussions, with each lecture or discussion accompanied by appropriate motion pictures giving examples of the topic under discussion. But, at present, opportunities for projection of motion pictures in the schoolroom are more or less limited to educational films. So, for our examples, we are forced to depend entirely upon the offerings of the motion-picture theaters.

We shall be handicapped in our study of motion pictures until it becomes possible to project the desired pictures upon a screen in the schoolroom. Not only should the best and poorest pictures be studied, but we should also have pictures made specifically for the purpose of training persons in the art of motion-picture criticism. For example, when a certain type of lighting is described, a scene demonstrating such lighting should be flashed on the screen. The class in motion-picture appreciation ought to view scenes which are photographed in various lights, some satisfactory and others unsatisfactory. When an unusual scene from a picture directed by King Vidor is mentioned, let us say, that scene should be reproduced on the screen. Fades, dissolves, and other types of shots could be illustrated from well-known motion pictures.

In the same fashion, there should be a series of reels in which comparisons of good and poor acting could be made. We should be able to see Lionel Barrymore purposely doing a poor scene, to hear the criticism and suggestions offered by the director, and then to see the scene after Mr. Barrymore has put the director's suggestion into effect. And there is little doubt that this type of training in motion-picture appreciation will be available fairly soon.

In addition to these suggestions, I wish to offer one concerning the need for good books on motion-picture production. At the present time there are only four or five books which the inexperienced person can read with interest and enjoyment. Every high school ought to own at least twenty-five or thirty books on the various parts of motion-picture production. Such books will be written when a demand for them is created. In the Appendix (page 233) you will find a list of books which should be in your school library, with a description of each prepared by Mr. William Lewin, chairman of the Committee on Photoplay Appreciation of the National Council of Teachers of English.

Suggested Changes in Motion-Picture Production

It is hoped that the methods outlined for the study of motion pictures may change the type of motion picture which patrons are offered. Changes like these will help to improve the present product:

1. The number of pictures made by each producing organization might well be greatly reduced. If every film were exhibited for twice as long a time as it is now, we would need only half the present number of pictures. And it is likely that, if the number of pictures produced were cut in half, the additional attention which would be given to the fewer pictures would double the usual size of audience for that picture.

2. Pictures ought to be produced for more than one kind of audience. Children and adults need different pictures,

just as they need different books. There should also be an increase in the number of pictures which deal with serious problems of life. We ought to have more films like "All Quiet on the Western Front," "The Wet Parade," "Cabin in the Cotton," and "I Am a Fugitive from a Chain Gang."

3. We need training schools for motion-picture artists. These schools should give training, not only in screen acting and in photography, but also in scenario writing and directing. There can be no continuous development of excellent pictures unless there is a continuous development of trained workers.

What would the medical profession be like if it relied today upon the training methods of fifty years ago? At that time the apprenticeship period was about the only method for obtaining medical training. The training of lawyers was equally meager. Today, however, no self-respecting profession believes that it is desirable or even possible to train its workers in such a fashion. In the motion-picture industry, however, we find that conditions for training are much like those of the legal or the medical profession of fifty years ago. The motion-picture industry, which employs more than three hundred thousand people and has an investment of several billion dollars, interestingly enough, depends almost entirely upon apprenticeship training for its directors and writers. Not only is this apprenticeship plan poor, but the opportunities for an able person to show his ability in the field of motion-picture production or acting are largely left to chance.

In view of the huge influence which the motion picture has upon the American public, it is not at all fanciful to look forward to the day when the state or the national government will consider it important enough to have schools which train motion-picture artists for their work. At any rate, it is true that up to the present time this industry has not realized that its financial future is closely related to the type of training given its workers.

4. The star system should go, and with it the intensive publicity that accompanies the building up of "fan" audiences for the stars. What would have happened to the drama if playwrights had been compelled to write for some particular actor or actress? Screen stars are "built up" not because the art requires it, but because this is a way of making money. The majority of motion-picture magazines merely represent a type of publicity for these stars.

Contrast with our star system the methods of motion-picture production used in certain foreign countries. In Russia, for example, the young man who so ably filled the part of Mustapha in "The Road to Life" is probably no longer in motion pictures. Had this film been produced in America, he would have been exploited as a star. Criticism of the star system does not mean, of course, that we shall have no persons who are continuously acting in films. It does suggest, however, that the public is going to demand good motion pictures first of all, and will see their favorite actors or actresses only when they play in good parts. In other words, stars will not be sacrificed in poor plays as is common at present.

5. A new point of view regarding the place of motion pictures in our scheme of living must be developed. At present motion pictures are made only for personal profit; they must be produced to fit the needs of people. Many of those needs are satisfied by laughter and gaiety and joyousness, which erase our worries. Other needs relate, however, to the abolition of war, to a new point of view regarding crime and punishment, to the more satisfactory distribution of wealth, to a deeper insight into the problem of a demo-

Tom Sawyer *Paramount*

We need more pictures of the same character as this.

cratic government, to an understanding of the Negro problem, and many others. Motion pictures must be constructed to fill both types of needs.

6. In the same fashion as the Little Theater movement has been successful in developing and producing plays, so something resembling it is needed in motion pictures. And it is coming. "The Fall of the House of Usher" has been made by one amateur group and Eric Knight, the well-known film critic, states that it is superior to the noted German picture, "The Cabinet of Dr. Caligari." A monthly magazine, called *Movie Makers*, has been developed especially for amateurs.[1] High-school and college groups can do a great deal in this field.

At Central High School in Newark, New Jersey, a movie group under the direction of William Lewin has developed a school newsreel. Narrow width sound-on-film cameras and projectors are now available, and these offer excellent opportunities for the amateur club. Once such groups realize the dramatic possibilities inherent in many life situations they will be able to do some delightful and satisfactory things.

For example, one can make a film of the town in which he lives. In Rochester, New York, there might be shots of the beautiful falls within the city, or the swans in the park. In Zanesville, Ohio, one could contrast the work of the old potter with modern methods of pottery making. At Berea, Kentucky, one could picture weavers at work. Birds and animals offer a unique opportunity for the work of the amateur. One might photograph the deer in a park, a circus parade, a robin building its nest.

7. Cycles in the production of motion pictures should be eliminated. We have had the gangster cycle, the lawyer

[1] This magazine can be obtained from the Amateur Cinema League, Inc., 105 W. Fortieth Street, New York City, at a cost of $3.00 a year.

cycle, the newspaper cycle, and the horror cycle. But, you may ask, what's wrong about cycles? Cycles are based on the imitation of successful motion pictures, and imitations are rarely successful. A story ought to be put on the screen only when some writer and director are anxious to tell it, and not because some one else has made a successful picture like it.

If the reply is made that cycle pictures are produced in answer to a public demand, one might well ask, "What public?" The only sure thing we know in regard to public demand is that the public wants diversity and is willing to pay for it. Further, according to Eric M. Knight, of the Philadelphia *Public Ledger:*

> . . . Hollywood magnates . . . seem never to learn one principle: that the "cycle" pictures do not make money.

8. The motion-picture industry needs more experimentation to keep it from going stale. The financial downfall of several motion-picture producers has been due to the lack of boldness and ingenuity in production. The motion-picture industry will not produce artistic successes nor continue to yield huge profits over long periods of time if future pictures only resemble motion pictures that have been produced in the past. The future of motion pictures will not be assured until they give us more ideas and better characterizations. People today are asking serious questions about the world in which they live. The motion picture, better than any other communication device, is able to suggest answers to these important questions.

The motion picture as a medium of art must get into closer touch with the times. There is little hint in the current motion pictures of the tremendous changes which are occurring in modern civilization. The motion pictures, as developed today, are far from being the social mirror which reveals the mind and manners of our time. The motion picture must rise to a higher level of interpretation and express modern purposes and modern needs.

AN IDEAL PRODUCTION PLAN

In closing, may I set up an ideal motion-picture studio? In the first place, its chief purpose will not be the making of profits. Instead, its goal will be the education and pleasure of the mass of the people. The persons who make motion pictures and who write them will be educated persons, trained in the arts of the motion picture, and they will see life honestly and accurately. They will produce far fewer pictures than under the present system, but their pictures will present variety. The pictures will not all be prepared for the general public, but the lovers of good literature, of scientific discovery, and of social policy will each have their share.

Since the major aim will not be financial success, motion pictures will not be made for the greatest box-office appeal. Indeed, our ideal studio will expect to lose money on some pictures, and make up this loss on others, just as any book publisher does. For you know that often a publisher will publish a superior book, which will sell to intelligent people but will not sell widely. The publisher knows that he will not make money on the book, and may, in fact, lose on it. However, the book will add to his fame and honor as a publisher, and the loss, if any, can be made up by publishing a different type of book, one written for a larger, but perhaps not so discriminating an audience.

The artists and artisans who make our motion pictures will engage in this work because it affords them a good livelihood and an excellent opportunity to do creative work. They will learn the important truth that huge sums of money are no substitute for a satisfied artistic conscience. They will make good motion pictures because it gives them a personal satisfaction which might be denied to them were they engaged in other types of work. They will get their satisfaction then in doing the creative work which the true artist finds most congenial to his spirit. They will look with amused contempt on those so-called artists who obtain their satisfactions in vulgar display of expensive cars, Hollywood villas, and all such glittering trappings.

In the words of Ernest Betts we may say that:

> . . . whatever experiments are made, in whatever directions they are made, they will only reach perfection as films where the artist-director looks at his medium as though it were his life, where the film is the first and final article of his faith, and he can find other interests in no other way.
>
> He will not say: "I believe in this, in that, or in any one thing." But he will make films and we shall know what he believes.[1]

Conclusion

Let us take a sharp look at these suggestions. Are they too utopian? too idealistic? Who will put them into practice, bring them about? Well, how about you?

This training in motion-picture appreciation has given increased skill in selecting good pictures by teaching you what to look for and by teaching you to recognize values. It has given you a background for your motion-picture experiences, and has shown you how to make those experiences intelligent and enjoyable. You can no longer be satisfied with mediocre films. If producers are not making motion pictures the seeing of which you can honestly regard as a worth-while leisure activity, then you should demand that such pictures be produced.

[1] Betts, Ernest, *Heraclitus or the Future of Films*, p. 96.

You represent a group of intelligent movie-goers, trained in the appreciation of pictures, and you have the power to influence the future of motion pictures. If producers discover that there is a demand for the finer pictures, they will make them. The demand must be first created, however, and you are the logical persons to do it.

APPENDIX

SUGGESTED READINGS [1]

Beaton, Welford, *Know Your Movies.* Hollywood, California: Howard Hill, 1932, 192 pp. $2.00.

The best American discussion of the fundamental difference between the art of the stage play and the art of the screen play. Interesting to teachers because of its challenging and stimulating analysis of the theory and practice of photoplay production in 1932, with many concrete references to current pictures in the light of basic principles formulated by Vachel Lindsay in 1915. Argues eloquently against the abuse of sound and the excessive use of dialogue. Predicts a return to the art and technique of the silent picture with music and certain types of rhythmic sound integrated, but with a minimum of dialogue.

Betts, Ernest, *Heraclitus or the Future of Films.* New York: E. P. Dutton and Co., 1928, 96 pp. $1.00.

An optimistic essay on the art of the photoplay, in Dutton's *Today and Tomorrow Series.*

Patterson, Frances Taylor, *Scenario and Screen.* New York: Harcourt, Brace and Co., 1928, x–232 pp., with 15 illustrations. $2.00.

An illuminating discussion of the photoplay under the chapter headings: author, story, continuity, titles, camera, director, scenario editor, producer, press, and outlook. Appropriate for high-school students in the upper grades, as well as college students.

Rotha, Paul, *The Film Till Now.* New York: Jonathan Cape and Harrison Smith, Inc., 1930, 362 pp. $4.00.

Discusses the development of the film, the various forms of the cinema, the films of America, Russia, Germany, France,

[1] Prepared by William Lewin, Central High School, Newark, N. J.

233

Great Britain, and other countries: the aim of the film in general and in particular; the preconception of dramatic content by scenario organization; the methods of expression of dramatic content by film construction, visual and audible. Appendices include production units of some outstanding films and their players, a glossary of motion-picture terms, and a bibliography.

The following books are out of print, but if your library has them, or if you can obtain them in any way, they will prove interesting and profitable reading.

Barry, Iris, *Let's Go to the Pictures*. London: Chatto and Windus, 1926, xv–270 pp., with 12 illustrations. $3.00.

Written just before the introduction of talking pictures, the book compares stage plays and silent photoplays, discusses the art of cinematography, the use of subtitles, film acting, conventions and morals in films, production difficulties, problems of public taste, and leading directors of America and Europe.

Pudovkin, Vsevolod Illarionovich, *On Film Technique*. Translated and annotated by Ivor Montagu. London: Victor Gollancz, Ltd., 1929, 204 pp. 6s.

Three important essays and an address on the art of writing, editing, and directing silent films, with considerable emphasis on the technique of *montage*. Comparable to Edgar Allan Poe's essays on the art of the short story in that the author is a master of the art he discusses.

A GLOSSARY OF MOTION-PICTURE VOCABULARY

"**Action**" [1]—The director's signal to the players to begin performing.

Angle Shot [2]—A photographic view taken obliquely.

Architect [3]—The technician in whose hands lies the design, erection, and furnishing of sets in the studio or on the lot (an outside set in the studio grounds). He is frequently misdescribed as an art director, a term indicating that he directs the " art " of a film. This, of course, is absolutely incorrect, except possibly when applied to the art films of the middle period of the German cinema.

Cam [2]—The device which operates the intermittent movement of the film in a motion-picture camera, printer, or projector.

Camera Angle [3]—The viewpoint from which a scene is photographed, the position of the camera being governed by the mood of the scene. Normal angle is generally reckoned as being four feet six inches above ground level. The position of the camera is always controlled by material composing the scene which is being photographed.

Cine [1]—A prefix used in description of the motion-picture art or apparatus.

Close-Up [1]—Scene or action taken with the character or object close to the camera.

Cut-Back [1]—Scenes which are returns to previous action.

Cutting [1]—Editing a picture by cutting out unacceptable film.

Dark Room [2]—Room in which film is developed.

Developing [1]—Making visible the latent image in an exposed film.

---

[1] Taken from a list prepared by the Society of Motion Picture Engineers.
[2] Taken from *A Selected Glossary for the Motion Picture Technician*, published by the Academy of Motion Picture Arts and Sciences.
[3] Taken from *The Film Till Now*, by Paul Rotha.

Director [1]—The person who superintends the actual production of the motion picture.

Dissolve [1]—The gradual change of one scene into another.

Double Exposure [1]—The exposure of a negative film in a camera twice before developing.

Dubbing [2]—Re-recording of all or part of a sound record for the preparation of a new master record, for editorial purposes, for changing volume levels or frequency characteristic, or for changing the recording medium (as from film to disk, or disk to film).

Dupe [2]—Negative made from a positive.

Exposure [2]—The placing of a photograph emulsion under the action of light. Quantity of exposure varies very nearly as the product of time and light intensity. The quantity of exposure determines the amount by which the silver halide or nitrate in the emulsion will be chemically changed (" reduced ") to silver when the emulsion is developed.

Fade-In [1]—The gradual appearance of the picture from darkness to full screen brilliancy.

Fade-Out [1]—The gradual disappearance of the screen-picture into blackness. (The reverse of fade-in.)

Feature [1]—A pictured story several reels long.

Film (noun) [2]—A celluloid strip coated with a light-sensitive photographic emulsion.

Film (verb) [2]—To reproduce a scene or series of scenes on film.

Film Gate [2]—Movable element which when in operating position, holds the film in proper position against the aperture plate.

Flash [3]—A short strip of film, of a few frames, resulting in a rapid visual image on the screen.

Flicker [2]—Occurs when the number of pictures shown on the screen per unit time is not sufficient to insure complete persistence of vision.

Focus [3]—The concentration of a light.

Frame [2]—A single rectangle of the series on a motion-picture film.

[1] Taken from a list prepared by the Society of Motion Picture Engineers.
[2] Taken from *A Selected Glossary for the Motion Picture Technician*, published by the Academy of Motion Picture Arts and Sciences.
[3] Taken from *The Film Till Now*, by Paul Rotha.

Glass-Shot [3]—A shot taken partly of a constructed set and partly of a representation of the desired effect on a sheet of glass, which is placed in front of the lens of the camera so as to coincide with the perspective of the built-up set.

Inkies [2]—Incandescent lamps.

Insert [1]—Any photographic subject, without action, in the film.

Interior [1]—Any scene supposed to be taken inside a building.

Iris [1]—An adjustable lens diaphragm.

Lap-Dissolve [2]—Made by double exposure or double printing on the same strip of film.

Lens, Wide-Angle [2]—Short-focus lens which takes in a wide field of view, from 75° to 100°.

Location [1]—A place other than a studio selected for a motion-picture scene.

Long Shot [2]—A scene photographed, utilizing the entire angle of the view of the camera lens, with the lens focused for objects at practically infinite distance. Long shots include scenes which are general in their character—scenes of wide scope; the general assembly; the full room with all characters included; full-length exterior scenes; landscapes with characters included; etc. For long shots, lenses of short focus—from two inches to about one inch—are generally used.

Masks [1]—Opaque plates of various sizes and shapes used in the camera to protect parts of the negative from exposure.

Microphone [2]—Device for converting sound waves into variations in an electric current.

Millimeter [2]—Equals one-tenth centimeter, one-thousandth meter, or .03937 inch. Abbreviated mm.

Multiple-Reel [1]—A photoplay of more than a thousand feet of film in length.

Negative [2]—Film developed after exposure in the camera. On the negative, dark and light are reversed from the objects photographed.

[1] Taken from a list prepared by the Society of Motion Picture Engineers.
[2] Taken from *A Selected Glossary for the Motion Picture Technician*, published by the Academy of Motion Picture Arts and Sciences.
[3] Taken from *The Film Till Now*, by Paul Rotha.

Objective [1]—The simple or compound lens nearest an object which forms an image of it.

Optical Axis [1]—The straight line through the centers of the light source, lenses, diaphragm, etc., of an optical system, to which their planes are in general perpendicular.

Panorama [2]—Rotation of a motion-picture camera in the horizontal plane, without changing the position of the tripod.

Pictorial Composition [3]—The picture plane provided by the screen, bordered by the margins of same, on which material is grouped according to accepted standards of linear design and cinematic principles of movement.

Positive Film [3]—Film on to which negative is printed, and which is projected on to the screen.

Print [2]—The positive after exposure and development.

Projection Distance [1]—The distance between the projection lens and the surface upon which the image is focused.

Raw [2]—Of positive or negative film, means unexposed.

Reel [2]—Unit of motion-picture length, about 1,000 feet of film.

Register [1]—To superimpose exactly. Any indication produced by simulation.

Release [1]—The publication of a moving picture.

Retake [1]—Rephotographing a scene.

Scene [1]—The action taken at a single camera setting.

Scenario [1]—A general description of the action of a proposed motion picture.

Set [3]—A structural erection of a room, a street, etc., in studio or on exterior, specially built to meet the requirements of the scenario. The building and furnishing of the set is under the supervision of the architect, whose sole duty is to fulfill the needs of the director.

Shooting a Scene [1]—Photographing the scene.

Shutter [1]—A moving element, usually a disk, which cuts off the light in a moving-picture apparatus one or more times for each frame.

---

[1] Taken from a list prepared by the Society of Motion Picture Engineers.
[2] Taken from *A Selected Glossary for the Motion Picture Technician*, published by the Academy of Motion Picture Arts and Sciences.
[3] Taken from *The Film Till Now*, by Paul Rotha.

Soft-Focus [3]—A picture taken through varying thicknesses of gauze or focus disk, giving on the screen a soft, misty effect.

Standard Film [2]—Has a width of 35 mm.

Still-Photograph [3]—A static photograph of some separate shot in a film, either taken during production or enlarged afterward from the film itself.

Superimpose, To [3]—Two or more scenes photographed on the same piece of negative.

Synopsis [3]—A brief description of a proposed film in narrative form, setting down for the approval or disapproval of the producer the potentialities of the theme as a film subject.

Take-Up (noun) [1]—The mechanism which receives and winds the film after it passes the picture aperture.

Take-Up (verb) [1]—To wind up the film after it passes the picture aperture in motion-picture apparatus.

Tilt [1]—To rotate a motion-picture camera parallel to the direction of film motion and in a vertical plane through the optical axis.

Vision [1]—A new subject introduced into the main picture, by the gradual fading-in and fading-out of the new subject, as, for example, the visualization of a thought.

Working Distance [1]—The distance between an object and the nearest face of a lens forming an image of the object.

[1] Taken from a list prepared by the Society of Motion Picture Engineers.
[2] Taken from *A Selected Glossary for the Motion Picture Technician*, published by the Academy of Motion Picture Arts and Sciences.
[3] Taken from *The Film Till Now*, by Paul Rotha.

INDEX

241